MW01225168

To Eugenie

Enjoy —

Best wishes

Ron Vaughan

The Sport of Life: Reaching True Happiness & Success Through Fearless Living

Ram Nayyar
©2016

If you would like to get daily encouragement by email on your way to success then go to
http://www.coachramnayyar.com/changeyourlife

Legal Disclaimer

Copyright © 2016 Ram Nayyar & RTI Publishing All rights reserved worldwide. No part of this material may be used, reproduced, distributed or transmitted in any form and by any means whatsoever, including without limitation photocopying, recording or other electronic or mechanical methods or by any information storage and retrieval system, without the prior written permission from the author, except for brief excerpts in a review.

This book is intended to provide general information only. Neither the author nor publisher provide any legal or other professional advice. If you need professional advice, you should seek advice from the appropriate licensed professional. This book does not provide complete information on the subject matter covered. This book is not intended to address specific requirements, either for an individual or an organization. This book is intended to be used only as a general guide, and not as a sole source of information on the subject matter. While the author has undertaken diligent efforts to ensure accuracy, there is no guarantee of accuracy or of no errors, omissions or typographical errors. Any slights of people or organizations are unintentional. The author and publisher shall have no liability or responsibility to any person or entity and hereby disclaim all liability, including without limitation, liability for consequential damages regarding any claim, loss or damage that may be incurred, or alleged to have been incurred, directly or indirectly, arising out of the information provided in this book.

Copyright © 2016 by Ram Nayyar & RTI Publishing
All rights reserved. No part of this publication may be reproduced or transmitted in any form or by any means, electronic, or mechanical, including photocopying, recording, or by any information storage and retrieval system.

Connect With Ram Nayyar http://coachramnayyar.com/
https://www.facebook.com/Coachramnayyar/
Twitter: **coachramnayyar**
Instagram: **coachramnayyar**

Endorsements

The way Ram bravely draws upon his own personal experiences obliges the reader to be honest with themselves in their self-assessment. He effectively leverages his years coaching high performers to provide advice that is both succinct and practical. I have all the time in the world for Ram as time spent with him always results in a growth opportunity.

Curt Harnett, 3 Time Olympic Medal Winner

www.curtharnett.ca

I've experienced Ram's coaching first hand. He has a profound ability to connect with people and get them to quickly initiate the changes in their lives that are needed.

Cameron Herold, Founder of COO Alliance

Ram Nayyar expertly challenges you to address your fears that block you from true happiness and success. Being the experienced coach that he is (Canadian Olympic Badminton coach) Ram takes you through wonderful examples to illustrate and support his concepts. Easily understood ideas but challenging to execute – just like any sport!

The Sport of Life: Reaching True Happiness & Success

An enjoyable, motivating, thought provoking read that will likely inspire you.

Barbara Hislop, International President of Variety-the Children's Chairty

The Sport of Life is the uniquely Canadian story of a proud Canadian - an athlete and coach who for years inspired a generation of young players to reach the height of their potential. Ram uses real life experiences to masterfully and simply explain how anyone can reach their own potential and not just athletes.

Erin Shum, Vice Chair of the Vancouver Board of Parks and Recreation

Ram has known me for over 12 years when I first started playing badminton outside my province. I have been lucky to have him as a mentor and coach throughout my badminton career and beyond. This book puts into words the lessons I have learned from him and connects his personal stories with his teachings. If you're looking for inspiration as an athlete or in any other aspects of your life, this book will provide you with the tools to reach your goals and dreams.

Alex Bruce, Olympian 2012, Pan American Champion & Multi Time National Champion

The Sport of Life: Reaching True Happiness & Success

In our world, there are rare jewels who are born to do great things, who bring confidence, solace, empowerment and positivity into the lives of others. Ram Nayyar is one of those rare jewels, a person who came from humble beginnings and through his experiences, became one of the most admired and decorated sportsmen in our country. Ram's well written book is a source of positive energy, wonderful anecdotes and a clear message, that all of us can achieve greater heights in our lives through positivity and strength. We absolutely love this book, and we absolutely love, admire, and respect Ram.

Ustad Cassius Khan, The Ghazal/Tabla Wizard and Amika Kushwaha, Kathak danceuse/Harmonium exponent - 'International Performing Artists'

Knowledge, experience and an innate understanding of the human condition are just some of the gifts that Ram will share with you in this book. I found it thoroughly informative and illuminating; I encourage you all to have a read and explore your own potential of success. I have no doubt his words will give you better understanding of yourself and how you wish to accomplish your life's goals through self determination and fearless living.

Pullela Gopichand, All England Champion 2001, Olympian

Dedication

I am so very grateful for all of the stars aligning and for the universe working in its mysterious way that I was able to get these words on paper

Particularly I would like to thank my Mom who has always encouraged me to keep pushing ahead regardless of the conditions and to my Dad who I watched as a young boy 'write' so I thought maybe I could too.

Also to my sister who has always been in my corner. Finally to my friends who have been such a big part of my life, I want to thank you all so much for being supportive, encouraging and my cheerleaders!

Editorial credit to my friend Kim Thompson-Pinder of RTI Publishing who made this book flow.

Additional thanks to Geoff Geddes of thewordwarrior.ca and my good friend Richard Freeman for helping me sort some thoughts with respect to this book and being an additional set of eyes to make this book the best it can be.

In Memory of David Folinsbee

This year (2016) I lost a great mentor to me. He was the man that first put a racket in my hand, the guy that gave me my first 'real job' and the man that I could call up anytime when I had something on my mind and seek advice from.

David Folinsbee or Dave as I called him was an exceptional human being who was literally Mr. Badminton to Canada. There are so many legendary stories about him that I could write an entire book on those alone. His ability to teach and guide were exceptional, and I will always remember the invaluable gifts he gave to me; for without his guidance, I would not have accomplished all that I have. Thanks Dave. You will be truly missed!

Table of Contents

Chapter 1: I Didn't Want To Hide Anymore

I could feel the blows on my body as these bullies beat me up again. Why couldn't they just leave me alone? Hadn't I had enough? Obviously I hadn't, because here I was again feeling the brunt of their hatred.

The funny thing is that even though the physical blows hurt, it was why I was being bullied that hurt even more: I was different from everyone else. Have you ever felt that way? Have you ever felt like you didn't fit in and because of that you were unworthy? That was me.

To protect myself I would stow away. My journey to fearlessness in life began with hiding from everybody. I would find the least-seen route to get home. I would wait until the school cleared out, and I became a master tactician at not being seen by other kids. I would engage my teachers with questions while everybody else left so that I wouldn't get beat up.

My goal in life, up to the age of ten, was to become invisible; if no one saw me, they couldn't make fun of me, and they couldn't beat me up. But it was hard to be invisible living in the Prairies, and being the only Indo-Canadian kid in my school.

I had a beacon, in that being Sikh meant having long hair. From a young age I remember other boys preventing me from going to the men's washroom because they said I looked like a girl. When you're five years old, it feels horrible.

"I'm five years old, and nobody likes me."

This was a hard reality to understand, and nobody could explain to me why it was happening. Even my parents couldn't - and weren't they supposed to know everything?

The First Time Things Changed In My Life

When I was ten years old, something changed. Some new kids came to our school, and they were 'special needs' students. Ours was the first school in my area helping these children integrate into society.

I am so thankful for how far we've come in how we see people with mental challenges, but back then, and I am ashamed to say it, we called them the retards. For the first time in my life, I wasn't the center of the bullies' attention. They had someone new to pick on: Ethan and Derrick. (Not their real names. Most of the names in this book are changed to protect those I care about.)

The attention was on these kids; it wasn't on me anymore. We could all pick on them, and I joined in as well. I didn't actually pick on them, but I was so relieved not to be the one picked on that I didn't do anything to stop it. So I was complicit with what the bullies were doing.

Do you have a Mom who always knew when something was going on? I did. One day, shortly after I came home, my mom noticed I was somehow different. She said, "What's going on?"

I told her, "No one is picking on me now. No one's calling me names."

"Why?"

"We have these special needs kids now. Isn't it awesome?" I was sure that she would be happy for me, but she wasn't. "You should be ashamed of yourself. Until yesterday, you *were* those kids. Don't you see how they might be feeling?"

"Mom, they don't get it, they're special needs!"

"Yes, they do. Those kids have the same feelings as you." My mom is a very smart person. She never told me what to do; she just pointed out what wasn't a good course. This forced me to think about it myself.

The next day, I went to school , and I made friends with those kids, knowing that we were all going to be picked on together. But at least I had friends, and I wouldn't be alone anymore. And I didn't care because they were the sweetest guys ever.

One day Mickey said he was going to beat me up. I was trying to be brave, so I went to the bus stop where he told me to meet him, and sure enough, he showed up. He was bigger than any of us because he had failed at least one grade.

He looked, and said, "I told you not to be here. I told you."

Out of nowhere, up popped Derrick, and he stood in front of me. I couldn't believe he was there. He looked at Mickey and said, "Mickey, all you wanna do is punch somebody. You're a bully. Well, it stops now. You can't punch him, but you can punch me."

So he did. Derrick didn't move while Mickey punched him and made his nose bleed. He just didn't move. Mickey looked at him, confused, and walked away. He had never had anyone stand up to him like that before. And that was the end of it.

I was so proud of Derrick. He had proven himself to be a true friend, and I wanted to thank him. I remember going home and asking my dad to get me a couple of bangles, the little bracelet that Sikhs wear. I gave them to Ethan and Derrick, and from that day forward, they weren't "retards" or "freaks" or the scapegoats that I could ridicule to help me fit in.

They were my brothers.

How A Few Words Can Make The Biggest Difference

Everyone has defining moments in their lives. They either change you for the better, or they damage something precious in your life. I have had both, but in Grade 8 something amazing happened. I had a teacher hand me a note, which I still have to this day. He called that little letter a "warm and fuzzy." It was just a hand-written note that my quiet sense of humor was very much appreciated in class, and that I was perfect just the way I was.

When he handed me the note, I was in a dark place. All the years of bullying had planted hatred in my heart, and I had become very silent. It was easier to be quiet and not get noticed, but those few words changed my perspective.

I went from being invisible to being the class clown. I always had to have a funny answer for everything. I learned that people liked that, and that they liked me when I was like that. It was everything my heart craved, so I pursued it with a vengeance.

Young Adulthood

As I hit adulthood, I wasn't sure what to do with my life. As I child I wanted to be Indiana Jones, so at first I went to University and studied Anthropology. Then I wanted to be a lawyer, but it was another pursuit that proved to be a game changer for me.

I loved badminton. I played it all the time, and one day when I hurt my ankle and couldn't run around, I literally stumbled across my passion: Coaching.

As I sat there feeling sorry for myself, a kid showed up to play. Since her coach wasn't there yet, I offered to help.

"Hey if you like, I'll stand in the corner and return your shots while you run around." Without even thinking about it, I found myself saying "try this" and "try that," making little suggestions on how to improve her game.

Suddenly, the child went away and came back with a piece of paper and a card she had made:

"Thank you very much for hitting with me. It was lots of fun."

A simple gesture on my part to help a child with her game, and a simple token of gratitude in return. But it was so much more than that. I made a small difference in someone's life, felt good about it, and in the process, it changed my life forever.

Thus began my coaching career, and I had found where I belonged.

Since then, I have:

- **Coached Olympic athletes** (in fact as I write this, I am getting ready to leave for another Summer Olympics.)

- **Coached people of all backgrounds,** abilities, and ages, from 5-80 years old.

- **Travelled to over 90 countries** and every major badminton competition.

I've reached the highest level of coaching that one can attain in Canada. At the same time, I have the awesome privilege to coach not only other coaches, but also CEO's of major companies, actors and actresses, and many others seeking to discover their best selves.

Here is what I want you to know; it doesn't matter how your life starts, but it does matter how it finishes, and you have a choice in that. You can choose to change. I started out a loser that no one except the bullies wanted near them. I was the kid that was different and stuck out like a sore thumb. I wasn't popular in any way, shape or form and yet I was able to rise above.

I went on a journey to find success, and in the process I found out who I truly was. Now I want to help you find real success and happiness in your life. I want to show you how rich life can be, and how to enjoy that richness.

The great thing is that you can start right where you are at this moment. All you have to do is be willing to change. Are you ready to start your journey? Are you ready to become and do more? Great! Flip the page and let's get started…

Chapter 2: Fear Is Killing Your Success

Rachel sat in her rocking chair staring blankly out the window of her room in the nursing home. Most people thought she was just 'out of it', but the reality was, she spent a lot of time in deep thought.

Today, like most days, her thoughts went back to her younger years, but they weren't happy memories. In fact the more she remembered, the more her soul filled with regret. One missed opportunity after another filtered through her mind and each one made her sadder.

She had been given chance after chance to do some pretty amazing things with her life like play baseball in the All-American Girls Professional Baseball League during World War II. When her kids were small, she would write stories and was offered a book deal by a major publisher. All these things she turned down.

Her children had been given opportunities as well, but she never let them take advantage of them. She always had some reason why they couldn't do anything. It had such an effect on them that as adults they slowly moved away from her. They were tired of hearing about all the things they couldn't do and now that she was nearing the end of her life, she was alone. She saw her kids once a year on December 27th as they came for a couple of hours so they could assuage their guilt over not visiting more.

She knew why she did what she had done, and as she looked back, she saw the stupidity of it. Why hadn't she seen it sooner? Irrational fear had controlled her life, but the revelation had come too late to fix it. Now all she could do was sit in her chair, staring out the window, waiting to die.

The Biggest Hindrance

Over the years of being an Olympic coach, and a coach to top business people, actors, and ordinary people, I have figured out the biggest thing holding people back from success:

Fear

First of all, let me clarify one thing. I am not talking about the rational common sense fear of things that have the potential to do real damage. Let me give you an example.

When my friend Kim's son was one-year-old, he was just getting tall enough to reach things, and the red burner on the stove fascinated him, and he kept trying to touch it.

She did everything she could to stop him. She told him, "No." She gently tapped his hand. She watched him like a hawk, but it got to the point where one day, she might turn her back for just a second, and he might get his hands on that burner.

So she had to teach him to have a fear of the heat. She put the burner on low, put his hand beside hers and lowered them both down until he pulled his hand away. She taught him, "That's hot. Don't touch." After that, the stove wasn't so fascinating anymore.

There is a rational, healthy side to fear, and an irrational side. Healthy fears keep you from harm by teaching you not to be stupid. There's a physical outcome to it, a physically negative result to what you're going to do. Let's make a big pile of leaves and jump off the roof into them. That's stupid. You don't know if the leaves are going to support you or not. These kinds of fears are what I call more rational common sense concerns, and they are 'ok.'

Irrational fears are definitely not ok. They prevent you from taking on things that could enrich your life. For example, if you have a fear of public speaking, you just won't do it. In the end, it might be beneficial for you, but you will do everything you can to avoid it.

So fear makes us avoid things. If you're afraid of flying, you're not going overseas to see your relatives, or you will be taking a boat trip (if you're not scared of the ocean). If you're afraid of the water, you're not going to learn how to swim. If you don't like critters, you'll never take a walk in the forest and get to enjoy nature.

You might never write that book or talk on stage or write that song because of what people might think of you. If it is an irrational fear, it's not a good thing.

If you allow it to, that type of fear holds you back from doing the things that could make you more successful. If one part of your life is held back by fear, there is a good chance that a chain reaction will occur and hinder other parts of your life as well. You will never grow because you are too afraid to experience the things that cause growth.

We tend to dwell on our fears of things that may have caused us some harm or discomfort, and it is irrational. In many cases, the thing that we perceive as harmful may never even have caused us harm, but we believe that it did.

For example; fear of rejection. You never ask a girl out because you are afraid of getting rejected, so you just accept whatever comes your way. You don't ask because you might hear "No," and that will cause you emotional harm. That notion alone has the potential to cause a chain reaction that invades the rest our lives and keeps us from 'putting ourselves out there.'

Think about it. Are you afraid to take credit for something you've done right? How about asking for a well-deserved raise? How about saying to people around you that 'I should be treated better?' Those examples are all rooted in the idea that what you are saying or proposing will be rejected, and the feeling of rejection will cause you harm, and the best way to protect yourself is just not to do that thing. In that way fear WINS!

That fear becomes our internal wiring, and it colors everything we do. It becomes this sort of phenomenon unto itself. Eventually, if you don't deal with it, it can paralyze you.

Causes of Fear In A Person's Life

Fear is caused by an experience that is either real or imagined. A person could have the real experience of walking along and being hit in the head by a falling tree branch and getting knocked over. Now they never want to walk under trees.

They've taken that experience and blown it way out of proportion. "I'll never walk under a tree. A tree branch might fall because it happened to me, once. It may never occur again, may never happen to anybody else I know, but it definitely won't happen to me because I'm not doing that again." That's the real experience.

Here is the unreal or imagined fear. You happen to be with that person that was walking along, or you happen to be the friend that heard the story of the day the tree branch fell and hit someone on the head. Now you think, "Oh! Tree branches are going to fall randomly on my head. People said so! I won't walk under it because I don't want to get struck by this tree branch." People believe weird things and make them real.

Why is there racism in the world? Somebody told someone else that a particular race is wrong. They didn't experience it; they just heard it.

In sport it happens this way: "Well, if you play that player, you're going to lose because they are so good." You have no idea how good they are. You haven't played them; you don't know if they're sick that day. You don't know if your playing style is something that is going to stymie them, but you're allowing that fear in because you believe what someone else has said.

Now you've adopted that fear, and if you don't have the tools to overcome it, then the thing you feared will happen actually happens, and reinforces that fear. It's called a self-fulfilling prophecy.

I'll never forget that great movie, The Princess Bride. Remember the Dread Pirate Roberts? It turns out that he wasn't really a dread pirate at all, it was just a title that was passed on from one person to another, and the fear of him kept growing through the stories that people created. The stories kept him real.

Why do people buy into these fears? The answer is simple, it's about winning or losing. You don't believe in yourself, and therefore it's easier to believe in something that's going to cause you pain because you don't have a belief in yourself.

If you don't believe in yourself, you may as well believe in something irrational, because this validates your lack of faith in yourself. It gives you the excuse you need, and absolves you of responsibility.

You are no longer responsible for your life. "Gosh, I can't do that. I can't stand in front of a group of people and tell them what I think, because everybody that does that gets laughed at and heckled, and people throw tomatoes."

What you're telling me is that you don't want to stand in front of the stage and talk because some part of you is afraid of people realizing that you don't believe in yourself. The fear of being hit by a ripe tomato is just an excuse.

Winning And Losing

People say "I don't want to fail." One of my favorite things to teach is that your love of success or your focus on winning has to be so much greater than your fear of losing.

We can have different words for them. We can call them success and failure. We can call them "being on the podium" or "finishing last in the race." It just depends on how you look at it. At the end of the day, it comes down to one simple thing: am I motivated by winning, or do I fear losing?

That latter is really powerful because it's a negative. You may not want to lose, and that is great, but do you want to win? Are you willing to do what it takes to reach your goals and dreams because 'not losing' isn't the same as winning? That's where most of society lives; I call it the middle ground.

There are a lot of people in that comfortable place called the middle ground. Being an Olympic coach for Canada, I talk with my athletes about things like personal best. We talk about things that keep them in the middle and why that isn't the place to be. I have often said that "your personal best is a poor measure of success if you set the bar so low that you can easily achieve it." You also cannot, and should not, compare yourself or your success with others. No, this is not a contradictory statement - if you buy into the fact that your definition of success has to be to shoot for the stars, but be able to land on the moon with happiness. That is, aim high, aim very high; aim to be the best, but do not judge yourself harshly if you don't reach your goal. Instead, be proud that you've made your best effort to achieve it.

There is an organization that's dedicated to funding Canadian athletes. It's called, "Own the Podium." Its sole purpose is to ensure winning athletes are rewarded. That means unless you win, you get nothing. People say, "Isn't that harsh?", but the reality is that if you're going to put yourself in the position of being a competitor, then you had better win.

The middle keeps us stuck there by making us not want to be noticed too much, as being noticed, being a 'someone,' means automatic criticism. What do I mean by that? Think about it. Anyone that is seen (in a good way) is usually successful at something.

People will have one of three reactions. They put you on an unrealistic pedestal where you have to meet their expectations to stay there. They put you down to make themselves feel more important, or they attack you to try and get what you have, without earning it themselves.

There is a fourth reaction, but it is from a tiny group of people who love you just the way you are and take the good with the bad. They rejoice when you succeed, and pick you up when you fall.

Most people sit in the middle because they focus on the first three groups of people, instead of investing their time and effort in the fourth group.

What happens if you win, if you are successful? There's a lot of pressure to win and succeed again, because if you don't, the first win was a fluke. So that pressure feeds us to gravitate to the middle, and that is a killer in our society.

An Attitude of Winning

Say you have an athlete that has worked incredibly hard, doing absolutely everything that they can possibly do. At a previous competition, they were in last place, but this time, they give it their all. This time, they don't make the podium, but they get a fourth or fifth.

Is that a win?

Sure it is. They put their absolute best forward, had nothing left in the tank, and did everything they could to win, but they came up short. There's nothing wrong with that.

You're not a loser if you don't win, but you're not a winner if you don't lose. What I mean is that this is an attitude, not a result or outcome. **I can teach you how to never lose and always win.** This is one of the biggest secrets I have. I wouldn't want to share it with just anybody, but I am going to share it with you, my reader. And once I've told you, you will never, ever lose again. In fact, you will always win.

Are you ready? Here it is.

Always compete with those that are weaker than you.

Think about that for a minute. You'll always win. **You'll never lose, but are you a winner? Are you a success?**

So what we're talking about is an attitude that says, "Where am I competing? What level am I competing at and who is my competition?" Your ultimate challenge is always yourself.

If you feel validated by winning and playing and competing against those who are weaker than you, then I suggest a bit of therapy and perspective and move forward from there.

If you're somebody that decides, "I'm going to compete with everybody else and compete with the best in my field, but mostly I'm going to challenge myself. I'm going to place value on myself and my ego as I compete with the very best. And I am going to win, and if I don't win, I'm sure going to try. I am not afraid of losing, because I don't care about it. I only care about winning. I'm going to learn everything I need to do to travel on the path to that success, on the road to that winning, on the journey to that podium, that job, that new skill, that goal or that dream," then you're a winner, and you have conquered fear.

Fear is not the absence of doubt. Fear is not the lack of good judgment. Fear is a belief. It's nothing more.

Can You Overcome Fear?

I wouldn't be doing what I do if I didn't believe that you could overcome fear. I believe in going towards the positive and not the negative. It's really about gaining confidence in yourself, and then you don't fear anything else.

For example: if you're afraid of spiders, remember that the spider is the size of a quarter and you're A LOT bigger, so take care of it. I know it's creepy and crawling and you don't like it, but guess what? It doesn't care for you either. Put it on a tissue and take it outside. Make yourself do it once or twice, and you will realize that you CAN do it.

In the middle part of this book, we are going to cover self-confidence and self-worth and what you can do to become the person you have always known that you can be.

But first, it is important to understand the types of fear you have in your life. Knowledge is power, and how can you conquer something when you don't know what it is? Over the next five chapters, we will be covering the most common fears that hold us back from what we really want: fear of rejection, failure, success, the unknown, and commitment. We will look at what fear is and what may have caused it in your life.

Make sure that you read each chapter. You may think you know which fear affects you, but it is not unusual to have more than one, and if you are unaware of it, it can continue to hinder your life.

So let's take a look at our first one.

Chapter 3: Fear of Rejection

Fear of rejection comes down to one very simple thing. **My best isn't good enough.** That can be true for you on so many different levels. It can be writing a fantastic paper in school and getting a bad mark. It can be training really hard for an event and not winning. It can be asking that person out and having them say no. It can be giving a gift, and not getting the reaction that you wanted.

With this type of fear, before you even do something you've already figured out what the result is going to be, and it's never good. You have already come to a conclusion before ever taking action.

When I see that happening to someone I say, "You've already figured out what I'm going to tell you, so why are you asking?" When fear of rejection is a part of your life, it comes out in everything you do.

For example, consider a guy that's going to ask out this girl that he's got a huge crush on. He goes up to her and puts his head down, he's kind of there in body, but is fidgeting and nervous. "So I was wondering... if you're not busy watching the paint dry or washing your hair or something else important like that... maybe we could do something? But we don't have to if you don't want to!"

With that approach, you're so scared of getting rejected that you've already thought ahead and are covering your bases so that if you do hear "no," you have an adequate reason to fall back on, "She said no because she had to wash her hair."

That's one approach you can take because your so afraid of getting rejected. The other approach is, "Hey, a great movie is coming out, (or a great new coffee shop just opened up around the corner, etc,) let's go!"

She can still say no, but when you don't fear rejection you will be ok with that answer, and won't feel the need to cover it with an excuse. You are totally okay with putting your best foot forward and hearing 'no, it won't work'; your self-esteem is not damaged by it, and you don't need to protect your sense of self.

It's All In What You Value

Do you want to know who never has a fear of rejection? Serving staff in restaurants. They come up to you, and say, "Hey, would you like a cup of coffee with that?" and you may say, "No thanks." Do they go out and impale themselves? Of course not, but you rejected their offer. The funny thing is, those same industry workers that will tell you they're petrified of rejection. Yet, they get rejected every day. What's the difference?

The difference is that they don't put any value in it. They don't put a value on that person having a cup of coffee or dessert, but they put value in their job and asking for a raise or asking someone out for a date. Their value system has made them more fearful.

Is your value system making you fear things you shouldn't? Did you read the first part of this chapter and think, "That is me!" If that is you, then I have good news for you. Overcoming this is as simple as making the decision to change your value proposition. You're going to ask this guy or girl out and if they say "Yes," great. If they say, "No," also great, go and ask the next one.

But you may really have your heart set on that particular person (or outcome). That is okay as long as you remind yourself that life is not about the outcome, but the process. You may get rejected but it's not your fault. They may simply happen to like people who are taller, shorter, have darker hair or whatever. The thing is that free will and chance play a giant role in outcomes. Learn that it isn't always about you, it's about all the moving parts that come together to make an outcome.

This example can be used for anything not just dating. Anything you desire must also be the right fit for you. If it doesn't happen, chances are it was never going to work anyway. I've learned this through experience personally, professionally and when working with others.

If you really value something, the first thing to value is yourself. You want to protect that fragile little ego, but the more you protect it, the weaker it becomes. Let it grow. It is less fragile than you think.

It's much like anything else you know. We become stronger by lifting weights. We become smarter by studying deeper philosophical concepts or taking courses or earning degrees. We do that, and we're okay.

We practice different types of musical instruments. If we're getting good at guitar playing, we're playing ever more complex chords. We practice, we get better in a way that's cool. But when it comes to our ego, we never practice with it. We never say, "Hey, here's my ego. I'm exposed. You can say no, and I can hear no." And is it going to hurt? Absolutely, it is. Is it going to feel right? No! It doesn't mean you don't do it, but it's not going to kill you, either.

By ego, I mean your feelings. It's your heart, and you have to let that grow, too. I know it's going to hurt, but you always feel sore after you do a big workout. You're going to feel sore after you get rejected. It's just a different muscle that's feeling it. And here's the fun part; that muscle that you need to work on, (your heart/ego/feelings) is a lot stronger than any other muscle in your body. So treat it that way.

You can bounce back with it a lot faster than you can doing a big eccentric workout in the gym. It'll take three days to recover from that. You can recover from rejection a lot faster if you allow yourself to bounce back. Feel it and get through it.

When you don't, when you keep saying to yourself, "Why did I get rejected?" That's when you get into trouble. Move on and let it go.

When you get rejected, it really doesn't have anything to do with you, but you think it does, and you want to find the answers. It's that searching for the answer that will drive you insane and cause more fear.

Why Do You Want To Find The Answer?

She rejected me because I'm twenty-two years old; because I'm only 6ft tall and not 6'1"; because I have blonde hair and she only likes guys with dark hair. None of these are things that you can do anything about. There are all sorts of reasons why people are rejected, and they try to rationalize it.

I love the example earlier with the waitress. Why didn't they want coffee? Was it the wrong brand? Was it that she said, "Do you want some coffee with your dessert," instead of, "Do you want some coffee?" She could drive herself crazy trying to figure it out, but instead she just goes on to the next customer.

What if you go for a job interview, and they say, "We were actually looking for an electrical engineer and not a mechanical engineer." "Ohhh, I got it." That's something different.

First, let's never fear rational rejection because this is something we can seek to understand. For example, if an employer wants a mechanical engineer, not an electrical engineer, or vice versa. Those are rational reasons. Don't worry about them too much as they are easily explained, and they will happen. You were under qualified, or you were overqualified.

The irrational cases, such as, "How come I didn't get invited to that party?" or "How come I got rejected when I asked that person out?" Don't try to figure those out. They just happen also, but the reason for the rejection doesn't matter. It has everything to do with the other person, not you.

Could it be as simple as they were seeing somebody else? Or maybe they've made the decision to focus on school or a career right now. If the tables were turned, and you rejected someone, you would know exactly why, but they wouldn't. Would you say to that person, "You know, you just don't fit the picture that I have in my head." Would you say that?

Maybe we should, but I doubt most people do, and if they do, I doubt that the rejected person understands.

So as we end this chapter, let me summarize. Rejection is a belief that colours everything in your life. Because you see yourself as not worthy of acceptance, you think you will be rejected, then you behave in a manner that prevents you from putting your best self forward.

You want to be able to absolve yourself of the responsibility of putting your best forward because your heart/ego/feelings are too delicate to rationalize that your best just wasn't good enough. Through this process you assure rejection, and your subconscious works hard to make your beliefs a reality, and whether you know it or not, you do things to cause people to reject you.

But…

It doesn't have to be that way! You have a choice; you can change your beliefs, and the later chapters on self-worth will show you how.

Now let's take a look at...

Chapter 4: Fear of Failure

Fear ear of failure interests me because I love defining things. I often ask people, "When you say you failed, what does that exactly mean? What does failure mean to you?" The surprising thing is that it can be entirely different for each person, but there is one commonality; they always describe a feeling.

They will say things like, "This is how I feel. I feel beaten. I feel down. I feel somehow beneath somebody else, when everybody else is happy, I feel sad, that's failure." For most people, when they understand that it is a feeling, they can see where these things occur. They happen in our professional life, and our personal life and they manifest themselves in all sorts of different ways.

Professionally

On the professional side, the first thing that comes to mind is, of course, career. Sometimes, it's literally the choice of career that can hold us back.

It can happen subtly when you're young. Your parents are sitting around talking about you; one parent says "Just look at him, built like a brick house. He's gonna be an all-star football player." or "Look at her, she's already five feet tall, what a basketball player she will make. Look at that one; he's smart. He's going to be an accountant or a lawyer. That one, he loves playing with animals and stuff. He's going to be a veterinarian."

Our parents impart that on us without malice or knowing what they are doing. They are just excited at the possibilities that may come from their children.

As we grow, we may do this to ourselves and within our group of friends. Can you remember those early conversations that you had with your friends on what you might do or become? Then we come to an age where we need to think of a career.

Now as we think of a future job, what is it that we see ourselves doing? Some part of us is thinking about all of those past comments and mindsets that we may have developed. We're not thinking of necessarily what we want to do, but perhaps what we heard we might be good at or what we couldn't do, and we base our decision on that. You may have been told that you would be a great writer, but have you written anything?

You pick the 'what' but forget the 'why', and you forget that you might not like to sit in front of a screen for hours a day.

Let's say you decided on being a lawyer. Was it something you wanted, or did it sound right, or were you 'expected' to become one by your family? Once you start down the path of being a lawyer, you've now got to think about working for a successful firm and what that may be like versus working for a less successful company. Do you start weighing out, "When will I become a partner? When will I move into a different department? When will I have my own firm? How big will my firm be?" and so on.

So your choice of career can be the starting place where your fear of failure comes in. If you feel pressured to choose a career that is not in tune with who you truly are, it will conflict with your values and cause you not to believe in yourself. That non-belief turns into the fear of failure.

The second way that fear manifests itself is that we are constantly trying to bridge the gap of, "This is where I am, and there is where I want to be," and we don't think we have what it takes to get there. So, we become mediocre.

We fall into the place called mediocrity, "I can be a lawyer that will slowly and doggedly work my way up the ladder. In time I will become a partner in the firm, and I will consider myself somehow accomplished because there are others who haven't done that."

You haven't accomplished anything! All you've done is risen to a place where you can look down and say, "There are people underneath me so now I feel important." But what happens if you never reach that? Maybe you never make the attempt. Perhaps you never take on the caseload. Maybe you never produce the revenue that gets you to partner.

Third, our fear of failure is manifested in the position that we occupy. The higher we go, the greater the chance of failure and the more significant the consequences, but also the greater the chance that we might succeed. So people settle for the middle ground.

That is the effect of fear. It causes our minds to settle for less than the best, and because we are above someone else, we think we are successful. We never allow ourselves to reach our full potential.

In the land of mediocrity, the person learns to say, "Well, I'm going to be a middle manager. I'm never going to be a top manager, and that's all I'm ever going to be, and that's fine."

Or in business, I have my little hole in the wall pizza shop. I'm not going to have a chain of pizza stores and I'm not going to make this pizza shop bigger, but I'll be okay with it as it is. That's all I want to do. I don't want to push this. I don't want the world to taste my awesome pizza.

You don't do more. You do just enough. This happens in careers and business. You enter into a career where automatically four years later, your salary changes. You go up another 50 cents, and your cubicle gets bigger, and you feel good about it.

You never push yourself, because you may fail, so you stick to where it is safe, where there is invisibility, but you still feel like you have accomplished something.

In Sports

As an Olympic and Club coach, I see on a regular basis athletes being afraid to fail. This manifests itself in two ways. One is where the athlete tackles a level of play they could not possibly have the chance of winning in. That way when they do fail, it's 'expected'; it is not a failure to lose in a pool much bigger than you can swim in, right? It's just a learning experience.

When I ask them about it, their answer is, "I'm too afraid to put myself in a contest where I have a reasonable chance of winning, because if I fail, it will confirm my belief that I am not good enough."

The other side of the coin is that the athlete always competes at a level which is below or barely at their level. That way, even though they are winning, they are not being challenged, but they feel a sense of satisfaction with those wins.

It's like in the movie Rocky when his manager only puts him in fights he knows he can win. In his mind he is protecting Rocky; really what he is doing is stifling further growth.

You will always win that way, and you'll never deal with the issue that's holding you back from actually moving on to what you need to be doing. You can sit on the fence blindly happy and think that you have done something great, oblivious to the GREAT AWESOME things you could accomplish.

Personally

In your personal life, you have friendships, family, and a spouse or significant other. Those are three different areas. The fear of failure will manifest itself in many different ways, but mostly in the way in which you manage those relationships.

If it's a romantic relationship, the fear of failure is thinking, "Well, I know I'm with somebody and they don't make me happy, but they're okay. They're not Mr. Right. They're Mr. Right now. I'll be fine with that. That's okay."

Also, we may never even get to Mr. Right because we're afraid, and too petrified even to ask somebody to be in a relationship because that in itself gives us a chance to fail. It opens up the idea that "I could be rejected. What happens if I'm rejected? Am I a failure?"

Rejection at the next level becomes a fear of failure which then plays a massive role in our relationships. It affects areas like honesty, because we are afraid that our relationship will fail if we say something our partner will not like. So we dance around the topic, keep it inside, or learn to ignore it. Believe me when I say that eventually you will need to deal with it.

We create certain stigmas that we impose on ourselves. It's not real, but you have imposed it on yourself, and now you're going to wind up manifesting that in the way that you communicate with somebody. That same communication was learned in our personal lives with our families when we were young, and we continue to do it.

Have you ever wondered why kids and parents blow up at each other? It may be because they have suppressed honesty for a long time, having been afraid of how it might have affected the person they wanted to convey their real thoughts and feelings to.

When we do these things, we act with a lack of honesty, be it in a romantic relationship, friendship or a family relationship. When we lack honesty, we wind up in a crisis sometime later in that relationship.

I've experienced this in my life. For a long while I had trouble dealing with various family members. They said things, and I heard what I thought they said. But I don't think what was said was heard, or what was heard was actually said.

This led to years of me being very evasive on every topic, not really wanting to engage or to share my true thoughts on anything. Part of this was my lack of communication skills and inability to say things without casting blame and hurting feelings. But the larger part of it was simply not being honest.

One time this manifested in me completely losing my temper and lashing out. The anger I felt was intense, it went to my very core. I remember thinking, "This isn't me, this isn't the person I want to be, why am I behaving this way?" That's when I realized that years of not being honest with myself and those around me had led to this explosion.

Since that time, I'm glad to say that I've learned many ways to communicate and be honest about my feelings on things. This has greatly enhanced my relationships with my family. Now I teach that skill to others. My mantra is 'what is said is not heard and what is heard is not said.' If you can remember that, your relationships will be more pleasant experiences.

Let me explain…

Fear in a relationship makes us very dishonest and secretive. It doesn't let us be who we are because we're afraid that what we say will be something that somebody else doesn't like, be that romantically, in friendships or with family.

How many times have you gone to a party that you really didn't want to go to? How many times have we put up with a loud-mouthed friend? We have to invite him because he's an old friend and you can't not invite Bob. Bob's got to be there. But Bob's a jerk!

When Bob gets drunk, he becomes a pain. But we're not going to say it. You can't say that to him because he's your friend. But really he's not your friend because you can't say that to him. If he *were* your true friend, you'd say, "Bob, listen. I want to invite you, but when you drink you become impossible to deal with."

But now we worry. We worry because what will Bob think of us? Am I not a good friend to Bob? These things are what ultimately wind up holding us back.

Your question should be, "How does this fear of failure manifest itself in our personal lives?" It makes us dishonest with ourselves because of what we believe will happen, and the reason we worry that somebody won't like what we have to say is, again, we don't trust ourselves. We don't trust that we're right. Sometimes, we have to say, "Listen, Bob's kind of a jerk, right?"

For example, one time my friend Lacey was out with Sarah who she considered a good friend, and Sarah had brought her friend David. Lacey didn't really know this person, but she was ok with him coming along. Unfortunately, this friend of Sarah's said some pretty rude and insulting things to Lacey and Sarah didn't defend her.

Lacey was pretty upset by the time she got home and decided to call Sarah and talk to her about it. This was their conversation, "You just sat there, as your friend insulted me and said some pretty rude things."

"Well, he was just joking," Sarah replied.

"Well, that wasn't a good joke, and you probably should have interjected. What your friend said to me was inappropriate, and I think he's a jerk. I think he'll always be a jerk. But it doesn't matter what I think of him. What upset me is that you didn't cut him off. You didn't interject. That tells me a lot about you." Since that day, their relationship has been strained.

Lacey realized that there was no real point in maintaining that relationship because she couldn't look at Sarah the same way anymore.

Lacey chose to not let the fear of, "Well, we should still hang out, or she won't like me," prevent her from speaking the truth. She doesn't have time in her life for those types of people. We should be the same. We have limited time in this life. Let's spend it with people that we love and who love us back.

It's Not All It's Cracked Up To Be

Fear of failure, whether it be personally or professionally, keeps us from experiencing the fullness of life. It causes us to sit on the fence, always looking at other people's lives and either being jealous of what they have or feeling falsely superior because we might have a little bit more. We're never content, never happy, and will stay that way our entire lives unless we choose to do something about it.

Now is the time to recognize that fear in yourself, and start becoming a person who is free of that fear.

Only three more fears left and we will cover the steps needed to get free!

In the next chapter, we will look at the other side of the coin, which is fear of success and the ugly lie that keeps you from your goals and dreams.

Chapter 5: Fear of Success

I t's funny how life works sometimes. As I was preparing everything for this chapter, I ended up having a conversation with a client about the fear of success. I suggested to her that her fear was not of failure; it was of success. Success has a way of putting us in the spotlight where we feel the world is looking at us, and that exposure can be very frightening.

Unfortunately, when you become successful, you're naked in front of the world. Everyone's just standing there saying "Look at him/her," because that's how success works. It doesn't matter where you find that success, be it on a sports field, literary forum or music arena; whatever form that success takes, suddenly you are the epicenter of your trade. When that happens, those that do not have that success tend to feel either threatened or short changed, and in turn lash out in one way or another at the successful person.

That scares people. They know that they become a target, and that people will take shots at them. Even though those that take the shots are just acting out their own insecurities and lack of worth, it doesn't help the person who is the object of their attacks. I explain to clients that it isn't the person being attacked, but the position of success they occupy. That is, if someone else had obtained the same success, these same small minded people would attack them instead. The only way they can feel better is if they make others feel worse.

My friend Kim is a successful author of business books. She first started writing them to help teammates in her company sell and recruit better. She was so surprised when the people she thought would be the most appreciative were the ones who stabbed her in the back and verbally put her and her books down. They were upset because of the attention and admiration that Kim got and her potential to move up in the world.

It reminds me of a herd mentality: it's ok to be at the back of the pack, the rest of the pack will like you there, but try to move ahead, and they totally change and try to block you at every step.

The Other Side

So that is one reason why people fear success; the other is having to do it again. That is, you now have to back up that success, you can't just be a one-hit wonder (although there are many.) To be truly successful means you have to hit it out of the park more than once. That too can be frightening. "If I win one tournament, it's a fluke. But if I win more than one, and I can win for a period of time, now that's success."

In the music industry we have the phenomenon of a 'one-hit wonder.' While we may like a song someone recorded, when someone asks, "What else did they do," the answer is, "Nothing, just that one." That mantle just doesn't sound good, does it? Many people who reach the pinnacle of something and achieve a real success realize that if they don't follow it up, the only place they have to go is down. That is, if you reached a target one month, you've got to exceed it the next month, or you're not truly a success. Make sense?

Lack of success manifests itself in that way. It says you're successful or unsuccessful based on your ability to reproduce that success. So the idea of being successful can itself cause a fear that you don't know how to follow up on a fantastic song, sales target or book you may write or anything else for that matter.

Finding Your Muse

Successful people tend to have successful friends. I believe that is not by chance but by design. My personal experience suggests that successful people support my successes as I'm not a threat to them. See, my success is in coaching, writing and motivating, while somebody else's may be in real estate, so I pose no threat to them.

The wonderful thing about this is that even if they were a very successful coach, they would still support my successes because they already have their own, and they aren't threatened by mine. In fact, perhaps we can work together on a project to help each other. The same would apply were I a real estate agent dealing with other successful realtors.

These types of successful people have come to understand that the universe is full of abundance, and I'm not their competition, I'm their muse. Successful people have successful muses.

People that live in fear and failure also have a muse; however, their muses are also full of fear and failure. It's fascinating to me that when I study groups of people, many times 'like attracts like'. Be it a reading club, activity-based group, or some other loosely organized group, people with similar mentalities bond together. The negatively charged groups feed on each other's negativity, while the positively charged groups feed themselves in healthier ways.

"Am I in a negatively charged group or a positively charged one?" If you can ask yourself this question and answer it honestly, you can begin to change your view of success.

Can You Be Successful & Happy?

Yes, you can. The trick to happiness and success is to say, "I am not attached to the success." You may be asking yourself, "How can that be?" It's simple. It's all about your idea of success and your attachment to the definition.

What does success look like and how does it feel? What comes with it? Is it being on top of the mountain? Perhaps for someone whose goal is to climb mountains that's exactly what it is. If so, they must also realize that they can't stay on the top of the mountain forever. They're going to have to come down at some point, and someone else is going to be up there instead.

This concept was taught to me by the holy men of India. These men give up all forms of possession and work on not even possessing themselves (their bodies and egos). They have achieved a fascinating perspective that I have been trying to live by for some time now. It is summed up in this little phrase: "The chair that I sit in today, someone else sat in yesterday, and someone else will sit in it tomorrow."

To understand this is to give up some essence of one's ego. For example, I am the national badminton coach of Canada today, but somebody else did this before me, and somebody else will do it after me.

The beauty of this concept is that it is totally applicable to every area of life. All of my work, my wealth, and my success can be lost. Should I be in fear of losing that success, losing that chair, losing that position? No, I am going to enjoy the moment.

The best thing to do is say, "Hey, you know what, it belonged to someone else yesterday, it will belong to someone else tomorrow, but today it's mine. Today, I'm happy about that. Today, I'm joyous about that." That's how you enjoy success. That's how you stay happy. You're never successful forever. It will be good, and then you'll move on.

The Pinnacle of Success

Here is another thing to consider; you will never reach the pinnacle of success because there will always be a higher mountain to climb. When you reach one peak, you will look over and see another one, and start working towards that. Truly successful people never stop learning, growing and accepting new challenges in life. Their self-worth is not based on achievement, but on personal growth.

A successful person doesn't define success or failure by a position or accomplishment or the lack of either. Instead, they understand that success is measured by the growth gained (which can never be taken away from them) while in pursuit of that lofty goal. Therefore, it is not what they get *out* of the goal: it is instead what *they become* by the process of achieving the goal.

So you don't have to be afraid of success. When you understand what success is, how it affects others and the fact that you don't have to be the best forever, you are free to enjoy the moment and live a fulfilled life.

In Chapter 6 we will look at the fear of the unknown and how it stops you from even starting on the road to success.

Chapter 6: Fear of the Unknown and Getting Started

Remember my friend Kim that I have talked about a few times in this book? Getting started was one of her worst fears. When she was younger, she would never put herself out there if anything was new or posed a chance of failure. What if she tried something new and couldn't do it? It would just confirm what she thought of herself deep down, that she was worthless. Thankfully, that's not the Kim I know now.

In fact, she overcame one of the 'BIG' fears that people have, which is to become an author and have everyone judge you by the words you have written. She has written and published many books now and sees the unknown as a challenge to be overcome, and not as something that paralyzes her like it used to. She also now loves to encourage new authors to take that same step and not be afraid.

Fear of the unknown is one of our most primal fears. "If I don't know it, I'm afraid of it" seems to be a common sentiment. "I don't want to open that box because I don't know what will come out of it."

It Comes Down to Three Things

This fear manifests itself in one of three ways:

1. You are afraid of making a mistake, so you never start, and you sit in the land of 'what if.'

2. You think you won't be able to accomplish something, thus making you a failure.

3. You doubt anything good can happen and already project the negative outcome of what could be, so you never start.

It's always fascinating for me to talk to an older person, or someone with more life experience. Often I hear them say, "What I really wanted to do was be an artist," when instead, they are a doctor. When I ask them why, they respond with "I didn't know if I would be any good or could succeed enough to feed my family." I say, "Yeah, but when you were 22 you couldn't have predicted if you'd be good or not. You didn't know what success was and didn't have a family!"

There is a story that comes from ancient Hinduism, where the god Shiva and his wife are arguing, and the wife says, "You're not very good with humans. The rich get richer, and the poor get poorer. How come that happens?" He says, "That's not fair, I give everybody an equal chance, it's just what they do with it. Watch, I'll prove this to you." So he conjures up two little bags, one containing diamonds and the other some food. A poor man comes by, opens one of the bags and sees rocks.

"Those are useless," he thinks, and so he opens the other bag, finds food, and says, "Oh my god, food!" He takes that bag and walks off. Two minutes later, a rich man comes along and exclaims, "Wow, diamonds! Awesome!" And he walks off with them.

"Now, did I treat them any differently?" asks Shiva. "I didn't. It wasn't what was in the bag. It was what was in their dreams, or what they thought they could do with what they saw. They created that reality; I gave them both an equal chance."

The fear of the unknown is: "What will I do with this opportunity before me? What if this or that happens? What if... What if... What if..." Instead of trying, and finding out practically if this is truly something for you, you spend too much time trying to figure it all out before even taking the first step. This indecision keeps us from achieving the greatness that is inside of us waiting to come out. Those who have reached success in life have learned this one simple principle; you only get there one step at a time, and many times you won't see the next step until you have taken the first.

Sometimes, we are also afraid that if we start something, we'll never finish it, guaranteeing our feeling of failure. How many times do we procrastinate? That is one of the main symptoms of the fear of the unknown. We put things off with excuses. "I got a lot of stuff on my plate right now. I don't want to start working on it, because if I start I'll only get halfway through, and then I'll feel like a failure and what will other people think of me?'

That fear is two fold,
One, I don't know what will happen if I open the door; I don't know where it leads, and that scares me because I live

in a make-believe world, so if I open that door and find out it isn't a good one, my make believe reality won't be real anymore!

The second one is, if I do open that door and I walk through, what happens if I can't finish that walk? What happens if I open that door and discover that I have to do a few more things than I thought to finish the task? If I don't finish, I fail, so, it's better just not to open it, right? So you find yourself sitting around at 80 or 90 years of age and thinking, "Why didn't I open that door?"

Remember, you can live in fear and doubt, or in anticipation and achievement; the choice is yours!

Learn From my Regret

I'm not a person that lives in or laments the past, but I do have one particular regret. The key thing is however, that I learned from it.

When I was younger, I knew a wonderful young lady, and we had some great adventures together. She was perfect for me, and I loved her, and I also lost her.

Why?

Because I was afraid of the answer to one simple question: "Do you like me as more than a friend?" Nine words held me in fear of the unknown, and I lost one of the true loves of my life.

From that experience, I learned to never wonder about the unknown, to never be afraid to find the answers to the most important questions in my life. I would rather know the answer and deal with it, than spend my life wondering what could have happened.

How To Conquer The Fear of Starting Things

There are a few different ways to overcome our fears and start completing tasks, depending on the situation. The best advice I can give you is that when you have a lot of things to do, write them all down, pick out the three most important ones and make sure you get them done. Just get three things done, work on them, and then work on the rest of the list. This simple trick will stop your procrastination. So don't put it off!

As you go through that, you will discover that your capacity to do things is a lot bigger than you thought. From my personal experience, I've learned that because I am not afraid of the unknown, and I'm not afraid to start things, I can manage two full-time jobs, a business, and author books like this one.

A Quick Tip About Fear

As we discussed earlier, fear keeps you from doing things, but here is a quick tip you can use to conquer any irrational fear. Feel the fear, but take action anyway. Feel it at a visceral level. Go through it all, including the nerves. I want you to imagine the most horrible thing that can happen.

Now anything else that happens can only be better. When I tell people that, they say, "I can do that. I never thought of that before; that'll work!"

Will there be times that you try something new, and it's not the right decision? Of course. We have all tried going down a road only to realize it is the wrong one. That doesn't mean you should stop trying. All that means is that you've learned from the experience and are better able to go down the right road.

Every successful person has made mistakes. The difference is that they don't become afraid. They pick up the pieces, learn from them, and find the path that does work - and you can do the same.

Next in Chapter 7 we will look at something that keeps us from fullness in life because it separates us from true intimacy.

Chapter 7: Fear of Commitment

Andrea couldn't believe that it had happened again. Here she was lying on her bed with her heart breaking more than she ever thought it could.

How could Thomas do this to her? She knew deep down in her heart that he loved her, so why couldn't he just tell her? Last Saturday had been the most amazing day of her life, and it ended with the kiss that she had been waiting 18 months for.

Now it is one week later, and Thomas has completely abandoned her. He won't even answer his phone. After a few days, she leaves a message, and even though she knows that he's heard it, there still is no response.

The first time he did this one year ago, she just figured that he was shy and uncomfortable with expressing his feelings, and even though it hurt, she was able to forgive him. Six months ago, when they started hanging out again, she thought that he must have gotten over it and was ready to work on their relationship. Now here she was alone again with a broken heart and a resolve to never let that happen again.

That was 26 years ago, but thankfully the story has a happy ending. A couple of months later, Andrea met a wonderful man who loved her with his whole heart, and they married. Two children and 25 years later, they are more in love than they ever were, and their commitment to each other is stronger than ever.

It Traps You

Throughout this chapter, we are going to look at different ways that fear of commitment can affect your life, but it really comes down to feeling trapped and seeing no way out. You feel like you can't change what your life will become. There is no flexibility. If I enter this job, if I enter this relationship, if I enter the situation, nothing will ever change again. It's that idea that if I walk through the door, I can never walk back out. So you never take that chance.

It not only affects relationships but everything you do. You will have a hard time committing to even simple things. There are a bunch of people in my life that have what I call, 'The Flaky Factor.'

On Monday, I will say to them, "Hey, let's meet up on Friday." and they will say, "Yeah, yeah, yeah, yeah." On Tuesday they will connect with me and say, "I'm not a hundred percent sure, let's reconfirm for tomorrow." Then you try to reconfirm each day that week. By Friday morning they say. "Just give me till the afternoon." and then something happens, and they don't show up. I have learned to distinguish very quickly the people I can keep plans with and the people that I can't.

When fear of commitment is a big part of your life, you may discover that you have a hard time committing to others in the same way that you have a hard time committing to complete a goal yourself. The thought that permeates is one that says, "What if my best isn't good enough?" Oh sure, you will have lots of ideas, but won't put any plans into action, thereby confirming your self-fulfilled prophecy.

For example, people often fear to commit to a workout regime because they may not get the results they wanted. It's so much easier not to start at all and say, "Workout regimes don't really work." Those types of people believe that if they don't commit, they can't fail.

Romantic Relationships And Unrealistic Expectations

The second major area where fear of commitment appears is in your romantic relationships, and it usually comes down to unrealistic expectations.

It starts when you create for yourself a fictitious 'dream someone.' In the meantime, you are afraid of picking the wrong person because your expectations are so high that there is never anybody who can meet them. You keep searching, yet you won't commit to anybody because you always think there's someone better down the road.

We live in a world that is constantly putting false images in front of our face and saying, "Oh, that's how life could be." It can't, because it's a complete and utter lie.

No one person can ever meet every need you have in life, and looking for someone who can, will only make you miserable. It sets you up for failure before you have even started. You will spend your life going from person to person and never find what you are looking for.

The reverse can also occur. You pick someone you know will ultimately be incompatible with your needs and desires. Of course, this will lead to some dysfunction in the relationship, which will lead to a breakup, and on and on the cycle will go.

Does this make sense? Your fear of commitment manifests itself in you being either over zealous or underachieving. It's so insidious in its hold on you that you may not even see it. Instead, you will say 'just can't find the right one' or 'they are all jerks.'

Unrealistic timing

I had an athlete say, "Coach, I've decided I'm going to train for the Olympics."

"Great, so which Olympics are we talking about?"

"2016."

"You do realize that it's 2014? That's not going to happen."

"Why?"

"Well, it takes a lot of time to do that."

"Oh, I just thought I could start now and still make it."

What I found even more incredible was that he could only practice once a week. To be successful in anything requires a deep commitment to that thing for a period of time, and if you are afraid to do it, you will never accomplish anything.

If You're Still Not Sure

Maybe you have read through this chapter, and you are still not sure if this fear applies to you. If so, read the seven questions below, and if you answer 'yes' to one or more of them, fear of commitment is an issue for you.

1. Do you always find yourself looking for something better in all areas of your life?

2. Are you always putting things off?

3. Do you always use the excuse that you are 'too busy' to do things, including developing new relationships or taking on something new?

4. When a new situation arises, do you always think about what happened in the past and then say 'no' because it might happen again?

5. When doing something new, do you feel trapped by it before you even start and thus you don't do it?

6. Do you feel vulnerable when facing new relationships, jobs or situations?

7. Are you always looking for that perfect person, job, project or situation?

If you answered 'yes' to any of these questions, congratulations! You now realize that it is time to change, and I have good news for you. It is possible to overcome this. It is possible to have deep, strong and committed relationships that grow over time. In the next chapter we look at the solution to the most irrational fears we have in life.

If you let it, your life is about to change forever, and you will finally know what it is like to be free. Are you ready? Then let's go...

Being interviewed at the Olympic
Celebration Parade Toronto, 2012

Multiple Gold Medalists 2011 Pan-Am Games Guadalajara, Mexico

Coaching at the Glasgow 2014 Commonwealth Games

Thomas & Uber Cup Trial, Los Angeles 2012
Ram & Alex Bruce

In the television studios at the 2012 Olympics,
with ladies doubles semi-finalists
Alex Bruce & Michelle Li

Inspired to walk through the beautiful mountains of Bhutan barefoot. 2004

With coaching colleagues Jeff White & Jean-Paul Girard. Commonwealth Games, 2006 Melbourne, Australia

Posing for my story In Maclean's Magazine.

**Sometimes you just need to be silly on a boat
Mekong River, Laos, 2013**

Chapter 8: A True Look At Self-Worth

The first section of this book looked at the major types of fears that people have in their life that hold them back from true success. We looked at what causes them and how it manifests itself in your life. Hopefully, that helped you to see areas of your life that you are ready to change. The amazing thing is that one solution overcomes them all: self-worth.

In The Bible, it says that love casts out fear. When you can love and accept yourself, fear won't be a part of your life anymore.

So What Is Self Worth?

Let's bring it down to the simplest explanation; self-worth is an acceptance of who we are and confidence that who we are is okay.

It's the ability to look at self, even be critical of self and still be okay. There will be times in your life where you're overworked, and you recognize it, but you don't beat yourself up over it. There will be times where you've gone out and partied too much, and that too is okay. It's the idea that you don't need to do anything to cause your happiness.

Happiness is where self-worth starts. There's that perception that says, when I do (blank), when I reach a certain point in my career or when I am successful I'll be happy. No, no, no. The truth is **when you're happy you'll be successful.**

I need to say that again. *When you are happy, you will be successful.* This is an important concept to understand. It doesn't work the other way around, and I've seen this over and over again.

In the sports world, we're constantly dealing with worth. An athlete goes out and wins a tournament, and suddenly feels worthy. The next week she plays another tournament, loses, and feels unworthy. Yet the act that she did in between was the same; she played and competed in the sport.

I ask that athlete one simple question, "How can the thing that gave you the happiness also be the thing that takes it away from you?" It can't, but that's the perception people have. It isn't the thing you do, it's your perception of it.

Instead, if you were just busy doing the thing you were supposed to be doing, and let the results take care of themselves, and not be tied to the outcome, you'd be in a better place, and you would probably win more because that's how it works.

I love using this example of a shiny new car and a person saying, "If I have that car it will make me so happy." Yeah. It will. For about a week, maybe two, maybe five. But at some point in time, it just becomes a car. It becomes a utility to take you from point A to B.

There are those that will say, "No, you don't understand. It's a status symbol. I've got this Porsche, and that makes me better than other people, and that makes me feel good." I'm going to suggest two things. First, that person is going to have a lot of things that can make them feel bad, because when I get my car, and it's fancier than their car, they're not going to be so happy anymore.

Second, you will never be truly happy in your life because there will always be something bigger or better that you have to have to be happy.

Self-worth is happiness in the absence of anything or anyone. As weird as that sounds, that doesn't mean that we shouldn't like people and have people like us, absolutely not. It means that we don't need others to feel worthy. We're okay just the way we are.

A Bit Of My Journey

For me to get to that place was one of the most enlightening journeys of my life. It was not easy by any means. I was ridiculed as a child for the way I looked; I hit that awkward stage as a teenager where I was different from everyone else. Being a Sikh meant I wore a turban and as I got old enough, I had to grow a beard.

In one way I was like most teenage boys in that my facial hair at that age came in all weird and uneven. Unlike most teenagers, I wasn't allowed to shave it off. Most days I felt like an alien and my thoughts were, "Oh my gosh, the world is looking at me, and I don't know what to do, and woe is me."

Then I became a young man and experienced the foibles that happen with love, like not knowing oneself, trying to understand how women think, being afraid to ask a question because you're worried that you're going to get rejected and therefore your worth is going to be affected.

Then as a business person or a working person wondering, am I doing enough, am I there enough? Even now, my identification is that of an Olympic coach. What happens when I am not the Olympic coach? Where will my worth be? How will the world perceive me and I perceive myself?

All of these are challenges that worth asks you to undertake, and thankfully, I've come to a place where I can say it doesn't really matter. I'll give you a simple reason why all these external things don't matter. The last time that you saw a nice car driving by you saw the car, you didn't see the driver, and if you did see the driver you probably didn't think much of him, especially if he sped by you, or took a wrong turn, or if you were having a bad day and didn't like seeing other people's success.

It's Ok to Be You

It's pretty simple. If we are going to be happy, we have to embrace ourselves just the way we are, be thankful for whatever odd configuration we have as a human. Our mindset, whatever it may be, needs to understand that you're okay just the way you are.

Now that doesn't mean that you never change. If there are things that you want to be different, you can change. You can decide that you're going to be more well-read. All it takes is a little bit of reading. You can learn a new skill or hobby. If you need to you can lose weight. The thing is to make changes that you want to make, don't make them because you think it will make you happy; just change because you have a desire (after you have examined it) and know it will enhance your life somehow.

You can decide that you're going to make more money, get a second job if that's what you need, but understand why you need it. Is it tied to your self-worth, because you need to accumulate more things to show more people? If that is the case, be careful because you're fuelling your negative self and not your positive self.

Understand that you're always fuelling something. You're always fuelling the negative self or the positive self. You have to become mindful of what you're thinking. Again, self-worth is the idea that I'm okay just the way I am, with or without people or things. It's ok to pursue 'things' as long as your worth isn't tied up in them.

It's A Process

Your self-worth is not going to develop overnight. It didn't for me, and it hasn't for anyone I have known or worked with. For years I would ask myself questions like, " Why doesn't everybody like me? Why doesn't everybody just love me?"

I was very concerned about what other people thought of me, and it took me a long time through baby steps to get to the stage of coming to a place where it doesn't affect me anymore. Is anybody completely self-worthy? I don't know. I still have my occasional doubts, and I still have my questions at times, but they don't last long, and I have learned how to handle them.

And that is what I am going to show you in the next chapter; how to build your self-confidence step by step.

Has this book been of help to you? Are you eager to learn more? Go to http://www.coachramnayyar.com/changeyourlife and put your name and email address in to get regular encouragement that will help you become the person you want to be.

Chapter 9: Activities to Build Self-Worth

Before we look at the steps, there are some things that you need to accept as truth before you can move on.

1. You Are Worthy Just The Way You Are

You have worth just because you were born and live on this earth. There is nothing that you can do to change that, and there is nothing that you can do to earn it. It is just a fact that you need to accept if you are going to move forward. For those who believe in God, it is knowing that you were created for a reason and are loved just the way you are.

2. You Are Unique & Special

There is no one else like you on the face of this earth. Even if you are an identical twin, there is still no one exactly like you. You have things that only you can bring to this earth, and that makes you special.

3. You Have Strengths & Weaknesses

You are not perfect and don't have to be. You have been given strengths that make you shine and weaknesses that you can work on and make better. Accept it. It is what makes you who you are and important to this world.

4. You Get To Choose Your Life

No matter what circumstances you have come from in life, you have a choice of how you are going to live right now, at this moment. You can choose to be happy or sad; you can choose to succeed or do nothing. You can choose to walk in fear or self-confidence. The choice is yours.

So the beginning of building your self-worth has to be accepting those four things as facts in your life. Once you have done that, you then have to work that out in your everyday life, and that is what the rest of this chapter will teach you; the daily steps you take to keep yourself strong.

Your Daily Activities

The first question to ask yourself if you're feeling negative or sad is; what is this feeling giving me? Think about that question for a second, what does a negative feeling give you? When I pose that question, most people answer "Well it doesn't give me anything." But I know that statement to be untrue.

I challenge their statement and say "But it has to. It's giving you something. I just don't know what." "Well, what do you mean?" "Well, you are upset and sad for a reason, and I don't know what it is, but it's obvious, because you've been exhibiting a negative behaviour. It's got to be giving you something because you keep doing it!"

Whether you realize it or not, you choose to live in those negative feelings. Maybe you feel safe there; it is your protection. You don't have to succeed at something because you have the excuse of how bad everything is. I'm not sure what it is, but I do know that those negative feelings are giving you something and you, at some level, like what they give you.

That's why I'm not a counselor; I'm a coach. I am going to make things pretty straightforward, and it may be harsh, but it will be direct and true because you are doing this thing over and over again. When you decide you don't want to do that, that's your first step.

When you decide that you want to move into a state where you're going to be happier and are ready to make a statement like, "I want to be happy, I want to be whole. I want to have self-worth, independent of anything or anyone." Then I know you are ready.

That independence piece is really important, because as soon as you say, "Well if you just help me get this then I'll be happy," I can't help you anymore. You are asking for something that will never make you truly happy.

So the first step is, I want to feel happy. The second step is saying, "I want to experience happiness independent of anybody or anything." The third step is forming and starting the process.

My Quick Reminder Trick

To change patterns in your life, you need to be aware of what is going on in your head during the day. The trick I suggest is seeing how you're feeling during the day by recording it.

There's a line that exists within everybody and defines how they feel at a particular time. That line tells you if you are feeling happy or sad. It's that simple. And the trick to that line is 'awareness.' Simply raise your awareness so you know if you are feeling happy or sad; don't go through your day like a zombie, instead be connected to yourself.

Get a journal, write it down and keep track of where you are on the line. I suggest recording it 5 or 6 times through the day and at the same times each day. Remember, there is no 'on' the line, you're either above it or below it. If you're below the line, you're going to have a few tricks that will help you get above the line. You have three things that you can use to get yourself back above that line: your thoughts, visions, and actions. You can use any one of those three things to help lift you up.

If it is an action, you can try jumping up and down with a silly grin on your face when nobody is looking; when you do that, it will make you happy. I've always challenged my clients to do that. C'mon, let's do that right now. I dare you! While you are jumping up and down with that silly grin on your face, try to think a bad thought. Guess what? You can't do it.

Another great way to change your thought patterns is through gratitude. When you feel below the line, consciously look for things that are good and that you are thankful you have. Very quickly, you will find yourself above the line.

The last one is to visualize. Have visualizations of how you want to feel, (yes, literally visualize a feeling, like what does 'happy' look like?) Now think, what is one small step you can take right this minute to materialize that vision? It's really that simple.

Something To Think About

You can do this. Don't let it overwhelm you. Don't think about the outcome, think about the process. Think about all the small actions you can take that will move you in the right direction. For example, this morning when I was very comfortable with my cup of chai sitting on my sofa listening to music, I didn't want to write, I just wanted to procrastinate. I was clearly 'below the line.' My action was to go upstairs to my office, look at email, type a little, then suddenly boom! I started writing and now find myself very much above the line.

Once we start to become observers of ourselves, we become addicted to that happiness. We will start automatically doing the things that make us happy and make us feel worthy. One day you will realize that you have arrived at the point where you are the architect of your life and your life has changed for the better.

All you have to do is be willing to take that first step. For some, it may be the hardest thing they ever do, but I promise you this: it is worth it, and you will never regret it…

Now that you have conquered your fears and you are building your self-worth, it is time to take a look at what true success is. Most people have been deluded into beliefs that hold them back, and it is time that the truth comes out and sets them free. So let's continue to the next part of our journey.

Chapter 10: It's All About Your Perspective

I am thankful for the teachers I have had along the way who have helped me learn what real success is in life. They brought clarity where there was confusion and peace into my life when there was stress; they allowed me to exhale.

Have you ever just closed your eyes, taken a deep breath and as you let it all out, felt peace and contentment? You're not holding anything in, and you're not tense. You're not worried. You've just exhaled. So if you want that feeling, if you want to exhale, then I think that the stories and success lessons in this book will help you do that.

One of the teachers who helped me when I was younger was a lawyer. I had just started coaching, and I was coaching his kids. One night they had me over for dinner, and I had an opportunity to talk to him. I was very distraught because I was 21 years old, and thinking, "I'm coaching, maybe I should go to law school, finish the thing off and be a lawyer."

He looked at me and said, "Why would you want to do that?" "So, I can have the big house and a big this and a big that." "Yeah, but you have something much bigger than all of that. You *impact* my kids, more than I impact them, so I suggest that you stick with what you are doing." At that moment, I learned one of the many lessons about what true success is.

Misconceptions About Success & Happiness

Success is defined in today's society by anybody but ourselves. We get to see what success is through the internet. We see what people are doing every moment of every day on Twitter, Facebook, and Instagram. The concept of success no longer belongs to us, but to the collective mind of whatever thing we are plugged into, at the time.

For example, is it successful when somebody that you don't know, where all six degrees of separation are in place, has gone out and bought a fancy new car, a new plane or some other flashy item? Does it diminish, enhance or affect your view of success for yourself? Just today I was watching, "Buy The View."

On that show, people are buying two bedroom condos in Vancouver, Canada for $7,800,000 and are portrayed to be 'highly successful.' So naturally, people think that is a success, and in so doing, our semblance of success becomes not ours, it becomes imparted to us by people that we do not know and have no connection with.

We are influenced by people who are so far from our core values, that it is between the sun and the moon and the earth but we think it is us, so now we think we need to find a two bedroom condo downtown for $7,800,000. Is that truly a success?

Is it you that came up with that idea of success, or is it an idea that was given to you and you don't even know it? We have to ask ourselves the question, "What about that (fill in the blank) makes us successful?"

The Instant Gratification Trap

Instant gratification is one of those things that seduces us to march to someone else's tune and define success by it. It can come in the form of things, experiences, or people. That is, we can desire a new phone, want to eat at an expensive restaurant or mingle with certain people to make us feel happy.

When the latest version of the iPhone comes out, there is a giant line up outside the store. Everyone wants an iPhone, and there's nothing wrong with that, but then two weeks later, our attention diverts to something else, and we want that new and different widget. Isn't that so?

This cycle will repeat itself over and over if you let it, and you will never be satisfied or feel successful because there will always be something else that you don't have. Think about what I've just shared with you and see if it makes sense.

Have you ever measured that? Have you ever looked at it and thought "Hey I just got a new widget, and it really makes me happy." The question isn't that it makes you happy right then, but for how long it will continue to make you happy. I promise you one thing; the quicker you get it, the faster that you lose interest in it because it has no value to you and likely never did, except the value that others placed on it for you.

The great urge of consumerism really holds us back from our success, because we don't actually sit and define it, and that is a really big problem. Does having things make a person successful?

Take some time, define it, have a look at why you want the thing you want. Is it something that is useful to you and will enhance your life or are you buying it so that you will look good in someone else's eyes? Something to ponder as you think about buying that next widget.

Has Technology Changed The Way We Look At Success?

Throughout history, people have looked for success outside of themselves. It's been that way since the first caveman walked into the other caveman's cave and noticed that he had the brontosaurus TV and he didn't.

The acceptance and widespread use of technology is a fact of modern life. It seems we are plugged into something all the time so that the ideas of the collective mind are with us 24/7.

When I was a kid; we had dial-up internet, so you might be able to see the newspaper from a different country, listen to a song and, if you were really lucky, maybe watch a choppy movie. Today we have high-speed everything, and the ideas of success come at us from every direction except our own. Our conveniences are setting us up for failure.

So What Is True Personal Success?

True success for me is knowing that I have given my best to a worthy cause, something that makes somebody else's life a bit better and, in the process, makes mine better too. Success is about who you are, not what you own or with who you hang around.

True success is having a deep sense of contentment and peace. That for me is a success, and I chose it, not someone else. I took the time to study myself and arrive at that definition, and perhaps others share that meaning as well.

Anyone can have that contentment. They can know that their actions have helped others and have given something to someone, however, small it may be.

It may be volunteering to plant trees in our local schoolyard or creating a business that helps the disabled, giving them a meaningful job. It may mean having a foundation like Bill Gates' and giving away a lot of money, or it may be as simple as uttering a kind word to a lost soul.

It doesn't matter what it is. At the end of the day, if I know that I have given something to someone, I can sit back and say, "Wow, that was a success." And that someone can be your family, your co-workers or a complete stranger.

What Is True Success Professionally?

For me, professional success is when someone comes to me seeking their purpose, and I help them find it. That is success for me.

For example, my journey started as a coach, where people would come to learn badminton. I would teach them, and if they got better, that was success. I then transferred that over to business coaching, working with executives, athletes and people with different backgrounds, abilities, and challenges. I help them find their own solutions, and seeing them find meaning and purpose is the definition of success for me professionally.

Consequently, as I serve those around me, my services bring me many rewards, not only emotionally and spiritually but also financially. I think of the words of Buddha, who said that "Money is like blood, it must flow."

In many cases, success is accompanied by an increase in income, and for a time, I felt that earning a good living was something to run away from. A dear friend of mine saw this and shared a concept from the Torah. He said, "Wealth is nothing to run away from. If you are in the business of helping others and begin earning more, it means you're helping more people."

How Do you Define Success?

A lot of us define our success by the things we have, not by what we become; by the amounts accumulated and not the amounts that we create. We define ourselves by a storeroom of objects that we have gathered, rather than that which we have given away to help others flourish. That's the difference.

You can move up the chain as a professional and be successful, or you can be a custodian in the school who helps a lot of kids and be successful. There are no rules to this.

So how do I determine professional success? I measure it by how much impact I've had on others and, if possible, how that impact positively affected my own growth and my own self. That too is success.

Can You Judge Your Life By Success & Failure?

It is tough for me to say whether I succeeded or failed in life because I've never really judged myself that way. One thing I learned as a boy was that amidst a storm, the mighty oak will often be uprooted, but a blade of grass bends over in the face of the wind, and the next day when the sun comes up, it stands up straight again. You may think that oak is successful because of its size, but it isn't, while a lowly blade of grass survives and then thrives after the storm.

I've done many things that, in the eyes of the world, would make me a success: I'm the only Canadian to have ever coached an Olympic medal round match in my sport. I have coached a woman to winning the gold medal at the Commonwealth Games; and have coached a team that swept the Pan American Team and Individual Championships.

But they don't make me feel any more or less successful because success and failure are two sides of the same coin. They are experiences.

By the same token, I don't hang onto failures. Instead, I ask, "What am I going to learn from this?" All of these things to me are experiences, and these experiences teach me what I need to know to succeed. Some experiences show me how to do things, and other experiences teach me what not to do. It's not about what you get out of a single success or failure, but it is what you become by them.

Working With My Athletes

On a day to day basis, I push young athletes to succeed, to win, to focus on their goal. I teach them about commitment. I tell them, "It is the process of your commitment to the winning, that is the winning itself."

Winning and success are your ability to put your best forward, perhaps not get what you want, but still feel fulfilled, and still get up and try it again. Be committed to growing and learning and becoming the best you that you can be.

My Own Athletic Journey

I was definitely a failure as a player, an athlete, in the sense that I didn't win any significant events. I didn't win any big tournaments. I failed. But I kept doing it, I kept trying, I kept playing, and the commitment to the process was the winning itself.

The fact that I was able to say, "I will play this tournament, am not going to win, but am still going to play because it is a test of myself," was a reflection of my own being. It's the way that I became my own sounding board. Just to see how far I had gotten.

Will I lose my temper? Will I not be fit enough? Will I not be strong enough? Will I not be fast enough? What will I not be? That's ok. It doesn't mean that I failed, it just means that it gave me a gauge or an idea of where I am in this great world.

That 'failure' as a player opened up the door to my true calling and destiny as a coach, where I have succeeded greatly, and for that, I am truly thankful.

Success Is Only Limited By The Potential You Don't See In Yourself

You have limitless potential. The only limit you have is that which you place on yourself. You put it on yourself because it is based on your misgivings and ideas that were instilled in you as a child. Things you may not even realize are there.

Limitless potential also doesn't mean that you will have everything you want just because you want it. Desire and potential needs work, so potential (desire) + work = results. You need both, and if you think you can do it without one, then you are sadly mistaken.

There is a great quote by the Roman philosopher Seneca that says,

"Luck is what happens when preparation meets opportunity."

You create your own luck. "If it is to be, then it is up to me" is a great quote I live by. In sports we say you have to be good to be lucky. People always say that Gretzky was just lucky. I think he worked very hard to be that lucky. It is a funny thing how that works, isn't it? The better you get, the luckier you get. It is that way with life as well.

Goals and Success

The challenge in life is to have a goal lofty enough that you are dreaming, but have a dream attainable enough so that you can accomplish it.

I see people as either under-dreaming or over-dreaming in life. Many people would say that they want to be a multi-billionaire, but if they knew in their heart that they didn't like the idea of owning or running a business or didn't have the attitude to attain such a goal, why would they say such a thing? Why make goals that are ultimately unattainable, especially if you know that from the outset?

In this case, the goal is too big. What people are actually saying when they do that is they don't really want that goal, but it sounds so good that they can be seen as wanting more than they are willing to do. So working towards a goal that can't be attained is a way of deferring other goals that can be attained.

What if a person says that they want their house paid off in a certain number of years. That's attainable. That just means that you have to work your butt off. Right?

But very few people attain that goal because it requires that you actually put the plan into action. The action is where we may start to stumble. Maybe we don't want to give up that night out, those new shoes or that lovely bottle of wine so that we have the extra money to pay down the mortgage. In that case, it's easier to work towards those multi-billions right?

So have a goal lofty enough that it's dreaming, but have a dream realistic enough that it is attainable.

Can Anyone Be Successful?

The answer is absolutely yes as long as it is *you* that determines what success is. The hardest part is to define what that means to you. What would you do? What will it be? How will it feel? What are those elements that involve your success? What does it look like? Can you describe that to me? And it is not as easy as saying, "I'd like to have a $100,000,000." Anyone can make money, but few people can make a life. And that is what will make you successful.

It All Comes Back To Perspective

Let's say in five year's time you have everything you ever dreamed of regarding success. Will it make you happy? Maybe for a time, but true success is not about achieving that "thing" no matter what it is. The idea of success is flawed when based on a fixed object that is not within ourselves. Our idea of success must rely on ourselves. We must be content no matter what is going on around us. We must continue to move forward with our goals and dreams, but not get attached to the outcomes; those outcomes, good or bad, don't determine our personal success.

Was this chapter what you expected? Were you expecting some pep talk that encouraged you to DO MORE, to set unattainable goals and kill yourself trying to reach them because someone else told you that is what success is?

My hope is that this book will free you of that and convey that it's you who determines what success is. You can do and be who you were created to be, live a happy, fulfilled life, and at the end of it look back with no regrets. That is a successful life.

Now in chapter 11 we are going to look at how your mindset plays a role in determining your success, and I think you will be surprised at how it all works together.

Chapter 11: It's All Starts In Your Mind

T ara sat dejectedly at her desk. She couldn't believe that she had been passed up again for a promotion at work. In her mind, it was her turn, and yet they gave it to someone younger with a lot less experience.

Yes, she was occasionally late for work, but she always had a good reason and what did it matter anyway. It's not like it's that big of a deal. Tara looked down at her desk and the pile of work that she still had to do. Ok, maybe she wasn't the most productive employee, but she always got it done around the time it was due.

She knew she was well liked by the other employees. In fact she spent a lot of time talking to and helping them; that should count for something. Shouldn't that show them that she would be a good manager?

As she thought about this, her mind went to where it always went, and that was to the outline of the book that she wanted to write. But no, she had to stop thinking that way. What would people think of her if she told them her real dream? They would just laugh at her. The only way to success was to move up the corporate ladder, and that was what she would do. She had to find a way to become more successful so that she could be happy.

She knuckled down for about a half hour and got some actual work done, but it wasn't long before her mind drifted to the main character of her book and how he would overcome every obstacle and win the day...

It's Your Life

It's your life, and it is your success, and it starts inside of you. As we discussed in the last chapter, if too much validation comes externally, it's not your success; it's somebody else's. That validity must start from within you. It goes back to the definition: what is a success to you? What is your dream for your life? At the sunset of your life will you be able to look back with satisfaction at what you have accomplished, or will you regret what you didn't do?

It All Comes Down To Two Things

You are probably thinking to yourself, "Success can't just come down to two things. It can't be that simple." For some people, it will be simple, and for others, it may be the hardest thing they ever do. Curious about what they are? Well, I won't keep you in suspense any longer. They are the processes or systems you have in place in your life and your mindset, and we will spend the rest of the chapter looking at how they play out in your life to create the results that you want.

First, let's take a look at the processes in our life. We laugh at Sheldon on The Big Bang Theory because he's does laundry on Saturday nights at 8:15, but that's his system. That's his process: Saturday is laundry day. On Wednesday, it's Halo night or New Comic Book Night and Thursday is pizza night (or whatever) —we always have pizza on Thursday.

Steve Jobs was famous for wearing the same outfit all the time (I hope he had several of the same outfits), and Albert Einstein never wore socks. Processes such as these form an integral part of our day to day lives and a base to start our day. Because there is no change in our daily routines, our minds becomes freer to think on other things. It is a theory that many subscribe to and follow.

There are two kinds of processes when it comes to our lives. The routines we put in place to take care of ourselves, and the systems we put in place to accomplish our goals.

Taking Care of You

For me, those things include the body, mind and soul, and the nourishment that goes in there. For the body, that's exercise, healthy food and preparation of food. I'm fortunate to live in a city that has a lot of farmers' markets, and I can go and get fresh vegetables and fruit and prepare good meals. In the absence of getting those good nutrients in my body, I try to pick wisely as much as I can. I also exercise, and as a coach that is important because I have to 'walk my talk.'

I'm blessed by having time to practice these habits on a daily basis, but many don't have that option. They may simply lack the time, or work in a setting that doesn't allow for movement within their work. For example, if you are strapped to a desk most of the day, the movement/exercise option will elude you. Or if you have to travel for several hours a day for work, that too will take a toll; in that case, you will have to create exercise and food preparation time.

The mind must also find nourishment, so to that end, I'm always making sure that I'm learning. Learning is paramount to success so make sure you are always growing! So whether you're reading on a computer screen, or you're reading books or watching documentaries or listening to audiobooks—keep growing!

The spirit portion, for me, can be described as meditation. Meditation is when you exhale when you find the space between your thoughts, where you literally are in a state of 'being.' You do whatever it is that you need to do. If that means some sort of prayer, do that. If it means being in nature, do that. If it means listening or playing music, do that. Or if it means sitting in silence and finding that stillness within yourself, do that. Whatever it is, do the thing that is most likely to quiet your mind and do it *daily*.

One of my doctor friends described meditation as a 'hobby'... he asked me during a very stressful time in my life, what hobbies I had. To my dismay, at that point I had NONE.

If you feed the body, mind, and soul, you're doing something right, but how you do that is different for everybody. Some people will sit quietly in meditation, while others would rather listen to an audiobook than read a book. Some people for their physical activity would rather lift weights than go for a run. Whatever it is you want to do is individual to you, but those three characteristics are universal.

The Routine Of Your Life

My friend Kim recently asked me a question, "Let's say success for you was getting that credit card paid off in a year. Do you think there needs to be systems and procedures in place to take care of things like that in life?" And it got me thinking about practical things in life like paying bills.

I see bills (and taxes) as necessary and never going away. That is, as long as you are living in a globalized economy you're going to have bills to pay, and you're going to pay taxes. So instead of treating them like a surprise, I approach them with a plan.

For example. I set a day in the week that all my bills need to get paid for that week. Other expenses need to be factored in as well, with another small amount kept as a rainy day fund, and whatever is left over becomes a discretionary fund. I've also got funds set aside to cover yearly or other scheduled expenses such as Christmas.

How many people think about having different pots of money for different things, for example, Christmas? Do you say, "Okay, I've got a Christmas fund." I do. I put money away every month because a) I love Christmas, and b) I know that I am going to buy gifts for friends, family, and charitable organizations.

I already know I'm going to do that, so why not put the money aside in advance, rather than waking up in January, looking at my credit card bill and saying, "Oh my God, how do I pay this off?"

So putting systems in place needs to happen before tackling the thing you need to get done, and systems also play a role during and after what you want to accomplish. Successful people plan their success and then take action on it, in all the areas of their life.

Mindset, Habits and Thought Patterns

Mindset is the repetition of habit. The things that we repeatedly do become our mindset. If you're a person that comes home and decides you need that double scotch because you've had a hard pressure filled day, and you repeat that procedure every time pressure is felt, you've got yourself a habit.

Maybe your day was dreadful, so you have one more. Then you have dinner, sit in front of that TV, do a little work, have a late night snack and go to bed. You wake up in the morning, and the first thing you do is you rush out because you're late because you are exhausted from staying up too late last night. You grab a coffee and go.

You sit at your desk all day. Because you didn't have time for breakfast, you decide to have a big lunch. Then you go back to your desk and work really hard the rest of the day and come home. As you walk through the door, you see that bottle of scotch and the cycle begins all over again.

Over time your mindset will become that of a workaholic who probably drinks too much, and your enjoyment becomes linked to booze or food or whatever it is and these habits become that mindset.

Remember, we are what we repeatedly do.

Do Thoughts and Feelings Play A Role In Creating Habits?

Absolutely. We are either reactionary or proactive. If you're reactionary, every time you have a feeling that is negative, your reaction and your feelings to that is also going to be negative.

I believe in this cycle. A thought arises. You can't control it. A thought brings with it a feeling, which is also something that you can't control. The feeling leads to an action, the action to an outcome. That result becomes stored in your brain as a chemical groove.

If you look at that cycle, you'll understand that because you don't have control over a thought, you also don't have control over the feeling that it brings.

Then there's the action. The action is sometimes the hardest thing to start because my mind will give me all sorts of reasons why I can't do the thing I need to do.

For example, the idea of writing a book is something that many people have. They think it's a great thing to do, to share their thoughts and ideas with others. They see in their minds eye a book on a shelf that someone looks at and gets pleasure by reading. They think of the content, they think of the book name. But how many actually take the time to do the writing? That part takes action, and that is the hardest part.

So let's say I do decide to write a few words, and when I look at them I think, "OMG, I will never have enough to say" or "what happens when people read this, they will think me a fool?" Or "there is no way I have time to do this because I've got other things pulling on my day like a real job, family, travel."

If you ask any good writing coach, they will say the number one thing is to simply write. To start doing what you want to accomplish. The same could be said for a person that decides to run a marathon. The trick is to run a few blocks first, then move to miles, a half marathon and then ultimately the marathon. The key is in taking action. We get paralyzed when we over think about how it is such a daunting task and bring out every excuse in the book to prevent us from accomplishing our goal.

The only point in the cycle of thought where you have control is your choice to take action. That's it. There's no other place that you have control. That's what we need to train. That is where our thoughts and feelings play a role in success. Understand, I cannot monitor the thought that pops into my head or the feelings that come with it, but I can control the action.

So I wake up, and my first thought is that I lack the time and energy to write a few pages, or that there are many other pressing matters at hand today. That feeling of lack of time and energy and the urge to procrastinate confirm my first thought. My action is to get in front of my computer and push out a few thoughts, to simply start writing.

Maybe it doesn't feel great at first, but it will start feeling better. The outcome of that is I've trained my brain to take affirmative action; I feel good, and I've reinforced a positive cycle in my life.

If you enforce the positive cycle enough, your actions, thoughts, and feelings will respond and become more positively based. If your actions are negatively based, then your ideas and feelings become negatively based. That's when you're in trouble because you're caught in a negative cycle.

What we are really doing is talking about you creating successful habits. Whatever your thought pattern, those actions will then turn everything around; even if the first instance of feelings could be harmful.

Remember, thoughts are followed by feelings which are ultimately enforced or changed by actions. They're always going to be there, so learn to make them positive!

It's a Process

Are you feeling overwhelmed now? Don't be. All these things are a process, and the great thing is that you decide the speed at which you want to change things.

Let's just start with this one little habit for today. Next week, add one more while you keep doing the first one; the week after that add two, and then four the following week. Before you know it, your habits are changing into positive, successful ones, and you see the results of it.

Sometimes, it is easier to change when you have a coach on your side helping you every day. I would love to be that coach for you. Check out **http://www.coachramnayyar.com/changeyourlife** and sign up for training and encouragement from me and you will also get access to me to help you personally in our awesome Facebook group.

In chapter 12 we will explore the characteristics of successful champions and the types of actions they take every day to become the best of the best. The great thing is that these are things that you can do too!

Chapter 12: Characteristics of Successful Champions

No matter what your dreams of success are, whether big or small, there are characteristics that you are going to need to have to achieve them. There will be times when you face obstacles, and that is when you will truly know if these characteristics are in place.

Before we discuss them, I want to encourage you not to give up. Don't quit on your dreams. Many successful people have gone through rough times and still made it. Check out this great list of individuals who overcame incredible roadblocks and reached their goals.

Derek Redmond is a British runner who was positioned to win gold in the 1992 Olympics in the 400m sprint. During the race, his hamstring snapped, and he fell to the ground in an incredible amount of pain. Determined to finish the race he limped along with his Dad holding him up and crossed the finish line to a standing ovation.

Michael Jordan was cut from his high school basketball team because he wasn't good enough.

Vincent Van Gogh only sold one painting while he was alive. He would destroy paintings in frustration because no one appreciated his talent.

Bethany Hamilton is a professional surfer, who at the age of 13 had her arm completely taken off by a shark. Determined not to let life get her down, she relearned how to surf one-handed and went on to win national championships.

Jim Carey was homeless for a period of time when he was a teenager and had to live in a van. His Dad would drive him around to comedy clubs in Toronto until his career took off.

Steven Spielberg was rejected by the film school of his choice. Twice!

As you can see, these people didn't quit; they kept going and they made their lives what they wanted them to be. So what type of characteristics do these people have? I'm glad you asked...

19 Characteristics of Successful Champions

Vision

A lot of individuals use vision boards. It's great to have a vision, but I'm more interested in why you have that vision. Is it valid? What makes it compelling?

Some people want money. Why do you want money? Because it will make you feel good? What about the money will make you feel good? Will it make you feel successful? How far would you go to earn money? Would you do something illegal? If not, then is money in and of itself a good vision?

In my mind a vision needs to be backed up by at least five solid points:

1) I'm going to do this because it means something to me.

2) The 'something' it means is valid because it makes me feel good.

3) The reason it makes me feel good is exclusive of anyone or anything.

4) But, if other people like it too, fantastic.

5) My vision is adding something to other people's lives.

The creation of this book is part of my vision, and it means something to me. I want to have my thoughts down on paper, so I can share these ideas. It feels good when I get asked all these questions, and I can hand them my book to read and then discuss it with them. I'm not doing it to get famous. I don't care if nobody else sees it. Maybe no one will, who knows? Obviously, you are because you are reading this book, but that was not my primary goal. There's a purpose behind it, and it's a real purpose: I want to help improve people's lives.

Planning

Plans are necessary because a goal without a plan is only a dream. You have to decide how you're going to get there. How will you get your vision completed? What are the different elements needed? For example, I want to build a company of people that know who they are, love what they do and want to share their vision. They want to collectively help other people. In order to do that, I need to find the right people, the right mission. We need to share in the vision, and we need to go out and help people. That's called planning.

Schedule

You have to stick to a schedule. You don't decide the year before the Olympics that you're going to go to the Olympics. You decide ten to twelve years before that so that you dedicate yourself every day to going to the Olympics.

Every day you're going to be working to gain the techniques, tactics, psychology and life skills required to get you to the Olympics. And if you want a medal, you have a different schedule altogether. Scheduling is taking your plan and putting it on a timeline.

Budget

You're going to need money to do what you want to do in this life; you're going to have to have a budget and stick to it. And you can't always be breaking that budget. Sometimes you won't have money to do things. Sometimes you'll have more. When you have more, then you need to save. That's a budget.

Grateful

Be grateful in this life. One of the fastest ways to be happy is to look at the things you have and give thanks for them. I do that every day, and I silently say, "Thank You. Thank You for this moment."

A good habit is to write down three things you are grateful for each night. It works. Do it. You can use it to make so many other areas of your life better too.

Want to improve your marriage? Every day, for a year, write down something you are thankful for about your spouse and then present it to them. It will change your marriage forever.

Gratitude is one of the greatest habits that you will ever form.

The Big Picture

See the 'big picture,' but don't ignore the small things. Sometimes we have a vision that's 'out there,' but we forget to relate to the little things in here. My company may have the vision of working with 'the big hitter,' but then I get the smaller clients that say, "Hey can we have some of your time?" I've also got to do the small and straightforward things that keep everything flowing. In the same way, every Olympian was once a kid in the playground. Never forget that. Keep your eyes on the prize, but don't forget the small daily habits you need to do.

Always Be Learning

How big is your library of books, videos, and audio recordings of things that you don't know about but are working on conquering? Successful people learn. They learn about themselves, they acquire new skills, they learn just for the sake of learning because it makes them better people. Never stop learning.

Work On Your Happiness

Work on your inner happiness. Remember that you have to be centered and happy to accomplish anything. Work on it. Use that repetitive cycle of thoughts, feelings, and actions that I taught you earlier in this book.

Most people don't know what makes them happy. Their happiness is dictated externally to them. It's driven by somebody else. Dictate it yourself. Do not let anyone else dictate it for you.

True happiness isn't always about the big things. It could be stopping to smell a flower in your garden or taking a hot bath with a good book on a cold winter's night. It could be watching your favourite sports team win a game.

What makes me happy is shortbread cookies and tea. So if I'm sitting in front of my TV, watching my favourite show and having a cup of tea and a shortbread cookie, that's happiness for me. So is listening to music, having a good workout or talking to a friend.

Unfortunately, a lot of today's happiness is tied to the things we get. "If I get this, then I will be happy." That's the unfortunate paradigm that our current society lives in. Let's not do that. Instead, let's learn to enjoy each moment. Remember you don't become happy because you have or accomplish something. First be happy and then you will have and accomplish things!

Big Universe

Understand that you're a minuscule part of this big universe. No matter how big your vision is, no matter how much you think you're going to affect the world, you're not even a speck in the Universe. So don't take yourself too seriously.

Be Active

As your mind can affect your body, your body can affect your mind. One of the easiest ways to get out of a slump is to get active. Do something you enjoy.

Take a walk with your spouse and talk, wrestle on the floor with your kids, work out, play your favourite musical instrument, sing a song or even go bowling. It doesn't matter what it is. Just do it.

Give

Learn the joy of giving. If you're ever feeling bad about your situation, go down to the Mission Gospel and work in the soup kitchen. Give of your time. Give of your money. Give of yourself.

Be kind. These things will make you successful.

Track Your Results

Measure your results. Record them. Write them down. Make a diary of them. For years I got away from doing that because I had everything on my cell phone. Recently I went back to journaling again, and I'm so happy that I did. I write stuff down; I doodle stuff, and I measure.

Measurement is an outcome. Remember the little trick I taught you earlier in the book, "Are you above the line or below the line?" You can't be right on the line. Above the line means that you're happy and below the line means that you're sad. If you're below the line, the next question to ask yourself is, "How do I get myself above the line?" It's all related to how you frame the question. Never ask, "Why am I below the line?" That question keeps you stuck there, so instead ask, "How do I get myself above the line?" and guess what; you'll get the answer! If you do that five times a day, you're going to start being above that line a lot more.

Pray/Meditate

Meditation and prayer can be anything you want it to be. You can be still and quiet. You can be out in nature and reflective. You can be listening to music. Give yourself some time daily to be and to commune with yourself or the universe or God or whatever you believe in. We know now that the more you meditate, the more grey matter that grows in your brain, which ultimately makes you smarter and happier.

Work Hard

Successful people are hard workers. This isn't a new philosophy; this is old. Keep your nose to the grindstone, and just keep going.

Stay Focused

Successful people are focused. People that are intently focused in life stay the course. I know that there are always distractions but say to yourself, "Nope, not falling for that today." Concentrate on the things that need to be done today, and if you have done your scheduling right, you will get lots accomplished in a day.

Hobbies

Have a hobby. I was guilty of not having one for years. Playing music, listening to music, organizing, sewing, cooking, —it can be whatever you want it to be, but have something that you can do on your own or with others. Better still, have options that fit your circumstances. For example, I take a music lesson once per week with a teacher, but, if he is not available or I'm traveling, I can either play music on my own or write a poem.

Make Decisions, Have Self-Control & Be Self-Reliant

Have self-control. Things aren't always going to go your way. Don't break down. It's okay. It will be okay.

Be self-reliant. Don't always go up to people saying "I need help, I need help, I need help." There's no shame in that, but you've got to be self-reliant. "If it is to be, it is up to me."

Be decisive. Make a decision and stick to it. Don't be the "paralysis by analysis" person.

If you work on these 19 characteristics, you will never have a problem reaching or accomplishing any goal in life and being happy and successful in the process.

Chapter 13: Tying It All Together

Wow, what a journey this has been! I can't believe it is almost over. Not only has it been a journey for you, but for me as well. So many times, I have tried to write this book and just couldn't get it out because of fear. So many times I would put it on the shelf, disappointed in myself for not even getting it started and now here I am, writing the last chapter.

What changed? *I did.* I finally got to the place where I knew that I had to do it now, or I never would. I also knew I couldn't do it alone. So instead of chastising myself and calling myself a failure because I didn't have the skills needed to complete this project, I worked with a professional and got what I needed to finally put the words down on paper that have been burning in my heart for so long.

I hope that you don't think less of me, but there is a lesson to learn here. Never let anything stop you from reaching the success that you want in life. If you need to learn something to arrive at the next step, don't berate yourself and think you're a failure. Get up, learn what you need to learn, and do it.

I want to share a story with you. One of the professionals that I went to for help with this book is my friend Kim. I've talked about her a few times in this book. For years she wouldn't write and when she did, she never believed that it was any good.

As a child, she was told by a teacher that she was not good at writing and should stop. Kim was heartbroken and believed what the teacher said and didn't write anymore. For 33 years, she carried that lie around with her and let it affect her life.

At age 40 she was given the opportunity to write for her business, and she had a decision to make. Would she give into fear or would she give it a try?

Thankfully, she gave it a try, and she has gone from writing simple blog posts to books that have been read all over the world. Now she helps others reach their goal of becoming authors as well.

It All Started With A Choice

Kim's life changed with a simple choice, and now it is your turn to make that choice for yourself. You can choose to create a truly successful life that is not dependent on anyone or anything to make you happy.

You can work on your mindset and create one that is geared to success. Then you can go back to chapter 12 and work on all the successful characteristics of successful people.

You can do one of the hardest things you may ever do in your life; you can recognize the fear in your life and get rid of it through developing your self-worth.

Fear Is Not Your Friend

If the only thing you get out of this book is that you need to get rid of the fear in your life, then I will have succeeded as an author. Fear is not your friend; it's the enemy of your soul.

At first, it tries to be your friend and convinces you that it is there to help. Over time, it becomes a tyrant that controls your life and never lets you go. It will keep you in bondage all your life if you let it. The great thing about fear is that it is only a shadow pretending to be real, and at anytime you can walk through it, to a new life.

In Conclusion

For a long time now, my goal has been to help as many people as possible live the life they deserve to live, and hopefully this book will help you take the first steps towards that.

I can't make the choice for you, but I can help support you in the healthy choice that you do make. Come on over to **http://www.coachramnayyar.com/changeyourlife** and fill in your name and email address to get my daily encouragements that will help you stay on the path to success.

I want to end with a quote that has meant a lot to me in my life and has helped me to become the person I am today. Hopefully, it will help you as well:

When I run after what I think I want,

My days are a furnace of stress and anxiety;

If I sit in my own place of patience,

What I need flows to me, and without pain.

From this, I understand that

What I want also wants me,

Is looking for me and attracting me.

There is a great secret here

For anyone who can grasp it."

~ Shams – I Tabrizi

What are you waiting for? There is a big, beautiful, successful life out there for the taking. So take that first step. Fear less, have more and be your own champion. You'll be glad you did.

Bonus Chapter 14: Ram's Poems

One of the things I love to do in my spare time is write poems. It is a way to allow my creative side to shine through and I thought that I would share some of my favourites with you. Some of these poems come from my own experiences and yet others are purely observational I hope you will enjoy!

Silence of Tears

The most innocent thing in the world is a tear,
It falls without prejudice, it weeps without judgment.

It runs down the chapped cheek
of the traveling lover;

Who after a great journey and
much separation meets his mate.

It burst from the gentle face of a child who is hungry,
And still, at times, it sits so quietly.

In the eyes of the philosopher,
lost in his own thoughts

And with all of this, there is one thing
the tear cannot do;

It cannot speak; for it has no voice of its own,
It is simply at the whim of the
person who holds it captive.

To be the tear of joy and not be able to laugh.
The tear of sorrow and not be able to grieve.

Just to be,
Only exist in the way others think of thee.

What a fate!
What a great fear!

Thou poor captured soul tear,
I cry for thee.

Music Plays In My Head

I hear the gentle songs that I heard when I was bold,

I hear it in my heart; I hear it in my soul

I see her face smiling at me, looking as it did

All those years have past, and it

seems like a blink of my eyelids.

When I hear the melody inside of me,

Melancholy do I become.

Is this really real, or is it just what I have become?

No matter what it may be, what's real

is the feeling in my heart.

I felt it once before, I think it was

when we were first apart.

And now the music again plays on,

My days are done, my strength is gone,

But no matter what time it is,

no matter how much has past,

When those chords are struck,

those feelings do ever last.

I Want You To Know

Have I ever told you how I feel?

How it is down deep and inside?

Well I've got no place to run anymore

And nothing left to hide

So I'm going to tell you what I know

The only way that I know how

I hope you will understand and

see the me for who I am

Just an ordinary man, with something to say

When you walked into my life, I really wasn't sure

How was it that I felt, a feeling I couldn't cure

As autumn turned to spring,

and spring to autumn again

The walls that surrounded my heart

began to fall like a pouring rain

You started becoming a part of me, you shook something

inside. I tried to run away, I didn't want to feel,

I tried to go and hide

I couldn't do it, then, and

I know I wouldn't ever again

My shooting star has landed,

My feet are fully planted,

So come with me, hold my hand,

and together we will see,

How wonderful this world can be

for both you and me!

Anger

Teeth Clenched, brows curled,

A burn in the pit of your stomach

Lash out lash out, something to hurl

Dark, alone, desolate

Nothingness, fear and hate

Alone, empty, misery, pain

Want to do something, say something, but won't

Anxiety, playing the same thing over and over again

Why do you hurt your self so?

Love

Kindness, warmth, compassion

A warmth inside to melt the coldest snows

A smile so strong that even in the darkest hour shows

Sun shines, Togetherness, all is a bloom

Everything, fearlessness and compassion

Togetherness, fullness, health,

Doing, showing, caring

Restful and still looking forward to what is anew

Why do you not share it so?

Chapter 15: All About Ram
Olympic Badminton Coach, Author & Owner Of Fearless Consulting

He was quiet and shy and just tried to blend in. But that was precisely what made him stand out....in the worse possible way.

When he was in grade one, boys wouldn't let him in the washroom because they said he looked like a girl.

In grade 5, there was a bet among the grade 6 kids to see who could beat him up badly enough that he would have to go to the hospital.

His first memory of grade seven was the grade nines holding him down and spitting on him.

No surprise that he started down a dark path. Afraid of his own shadow. Even quieter and more reclusive. He also began to doubt... to hate...and to harbour ill will.

Then in grade 8 something happened. A teacher came along who told him that he was perfect… just the way he was. Over time, he began to believe it and set about changing his life.

He lost doubt and found hope.
He abandoned hate and adopted love.
Finally, he emerged from the darkness of his past and embraced self-acceptance.

I scorned him, belittled him, but ultimately came to admire him and respect his uniqueness. And I realized that in the end, he is someone I can't live without. For he is ME.

Ram's Accomplishments

Certified Level 5 Coach (highest level possible in Canada), Earned a High Performance Coaching Diploma and Chartered Professional Coach designations
Named Coach of the year - Manitoba (1999), BC (2001), Canada (2008)
Via Sport High Performance Coach for overall sport (2015)

Has Participated In As A Coach/Team Leader (Multiple Times)
Thomas Uber Cup
Suidarman Cup
World Championships
Commonwealth Youth Games
Youth Olympics
Commonwealth Games
Pan American Games
Olympics

Has successfully coached the only woman to have won a gold medal at the Commonwealth Games (Glasgow 2014) in Ladies Singles for Canada

The only Canadian Badminton Coach to have coached athletes in the Medal rounds of the Olympic Games (London 2012)

Recipient of the Queen's Diamond Jubilee Medal

Author of The Sport of Life: Reaching True Success and Happiness Through Fearless Living

Well known in every continent around the world as an international, leading coach, not only to athletes, but to high level business managers/CEO's and actors as well.

Connect With Ram

If you would like to connect with Ram for personal coaching or to have speak at your event then go to:

http://CoachRamNayyar.com/
https://www.facebook.com/Coachramnayyar/
Twitter: **coachramnayyar**
Instagram: **coachramnayyar**

Made in Canada
Burnaby, BC
13 December 2016